110662892

SABBATH IN THE SUBURBS

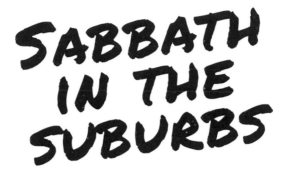

SABBATH IN THE SUBURBS

A Family's Experiment with Holy Time

MaryAnn McKibben Dana

CHALICE
PRESS

ST. LOUIS, MISSOURI

Copyright ©2012 by MaryAnn McKibben Dana.

Excerpt from "Holy as a Day is Spent" by Carrie Newcomer used with permission. Copyright © 2002 by Carrie Newcomer. All rights reserved.

Excerpt from "Marcus Millsap: School Day Afternoon," by Dave Etter used with permission. Copyright © 1983 by David Etter. All rights reserved.

All rights reserved. For permission to reuse content, please contact Copyright Clearance Center, 222 Rosewood Drive, Danvers, MA 01923, (978) 750-8400, www.copyright.com.

Bible quotations, unless otherwise noted, are from the *New Revised Standard Version Bible*, copyright 1989, Division of Christian Education of the National Council of the Churches of Christ in the United States of America. Used by permission. All rights reserved.

Cover and interior design: Scribe Inc.

www.chalicepress.com

10 9 8 7 6 5 4 3 2   14   15   16   17

Print: 9780827235212   EPUB: 9780827235229   EPDF: 9780827235236

Library of Congress Cataloging-in-Publication Data

McKibben Dana, MaryAnn.
Sabbath in the suburbs : a family's experiment with holy time / by Mary-Ann McKibben Dana.
   p. cm.
Includes bibliographical references and index.
ISBN 978-0-8272-3521-2 (alk. paper)
1. Spiritual biography. I. Title.
BL72.M365 2012
263'.1–dc23   2012028176

Printed in United States of America

For Robert

Go to sabbathinthesuburbs.com to download FREE thought-provoking videos, a free discussion guide, suggestions for group activities and retreats, and other goodies for book clubs and Sunday school classes.

Contents

Acknowledgments

I give thanks for my family:

. . . for Robert, my working week and my Sunday rest.

. . . for Caroline, little she-who-is; Margaret, the divine miss M; and sweet baby James; you make me a happy mama, every day. The song goes on and on.

. . . and for Mamala, an indescribable gift to us all, even when she spoils the kids with donuts.

Thanks to the Writing Revs for their friendship, encouragement, and sharp eyes: Ruth Everhart; Leslie Klingensmith; Carol Howard Merritt; Susan Graceson; Elizabeth Evans Hagan; Jan Edmiston, our member emerita; and Karen Blomberg, on another shore and in a greater light.

Thank you, Martha Lee Fugate, for gently pouring pumped breast milk down the throat of a bottle-averse baby so I could go to my first writing workshop . . . and for countless acts of friendship toward me and my children since then. I can honestly say that there would be no book without you.

Thank you to the Columbia Theological Seminary community that formed me in ministry, particularly Anna Carter Florence, mentor and friend, and Julie Johnson, who understands Sabbath on a deep level . . . and who also happens to be the Creek. To the congregations I have served as pastor, Idylwood Presbyterian and Burke Presbyterian: thank you for letting me grow along with you. To the Well, what can I say . . . I'll win that trophy someday.

To the folks at the Collegeville Institute in Minnesota and the Porches Writing Retreat in Norwood, Virginia: not only did I get tremendous work done in these places, but they are now what I picture when I need to go to my "happy place." (Those, and the Peter Pan ride at Magic Kingdom.)

Thank you to so many friends and family for walking with me: Gini Norris-Lane; my siblings; Margee Iddings; Keith Snyder; all the readers of the Blue Room; the dedicated staff at Chalice Press; my intrepid editor, Mick Silva; Manya Newton Lisse; Sari Fordham; Cindy Rigby; and the fierce and fabulous RevGalBlogPals and YCWs.

Thanks to Anne Fisher and Liz Dana, who hiked the mountain with me, which turns out to be the best preparation for writing a book I've found; to Gregg Dana, for being a steady presence and fathering my incredible husband; and Mary Caroline and David Mitchell, for moral support and Robert backup while I went on writing retreats. The importance of the pa-cakes cannot be overstated.

Dad, you're the reason why the words are in me.

A Note to the Reader

When you get to the heart of it, we were looking for a way to cheat time.

From the moment my husband and I became parents, we were told, "Don't blink. It goes by so fast." But in the hazy glow of maternity and paternity leave, we found this impossible to believe. Days with a newborn stretched out into seemingly endless expanses of time. She nursed a dozen times a day, sometimes for an hour or more. Robert and I took turns rocking her for long stretches of the evening. We went for meandering walks pushing the stroller. We watched her sleep. We marched back and forth with her on our shoulders as she wailed, a cry so loud I'm sure it's still reverberating in some parallel universe. Diaper changes, baths—all were slow and sometimes fumbling thanks to our inexperience. We rarely multitasked.

New parenthood was exhausting—an all-encompassing job that sometimes overwhelmed us. But one thing it wasn't was fleeting. The days were long. We were awash in time.

Parental leave ended soon enough and we went back to work. The baby's face kept changing overnight. Then she rolled over, gummed soggy crackers, walked, went to daycare, boarded the school bus. Without warning, those long hours together had shrunk down to a few snatches of time: at the breakfast table, after school, at bedtime, and on weekends. Caroline also gained a sister and a brother, and the process repeated, but there was even less opportunity to cherish the passage of time.

At last we understood what everyone had been saying. It does go by fast. And we want our children to grow up. But was there a way to slow things down a little? To breathe, bask, and behold?

Our Sabbath project grew out of a desire to reclaim some of the unhurried wonder of those early days of parenthood—to see what would happen if, on one day out of seven, we stopped working, striving, and hurrying. The result of this experience was clarifying, expansive, and freeing. It was also annoying, difficult, and odd. Our house was a perpetual wreck. We fell behind on work and domestic tasks. Our day-long togetherness sometimes drove us crazy.

Yet we wouldn't trade the experience for anything.

This book is for anyone who wants to learn to live at a savoring pace, especially in the company of family and loved ones. It's for parents who look around at the arms race of activities, sports, enrichment, and homework, and who feel a sense of unease amid all the good intentions and hard work. It's for people like a friend of mine, who looked up one day and noticed that it had been four months since her family had a day without anything on the calendar.

This book is for committed Christians, for whom Sabbath is a familiar concept, though perhaps not practiced much anymore. It's also for folks who grew up Christian but who no longer adhere to that faith, for people of other religious traditions, and for those who are suspicious of religion altogether. Though I write from a Christian perspective, I meet people every day from all walks of life who sense something dysfunctional about the pace at which many of us live. The longing to slow down, take stock, and experience delight transcends spiritual boundaries.

Each chapter chronicles our triumphs and struggles during a particular month of the project, along with practical wisdom and advice. Several chapters contain tips or tricks that helped us make Sabbath more pleasant and kid-friendly, called "Sabbath Hacks." A hack, whether in computer programming or life, is an "inelegant but effective solution to a problem." This Wikipedia definition sums up our Sabbath practice: imperfect and cobbled together.

When we began our year of Sabbath, we started with a simple rule: no work one day a week. This guideline seemed elegant in its simplicity but inadequate. In practice, we found our definition of Sabbath changing often as circumstances changed. To describe the evolution of our thinking about Sabbath, each chapter contains a section called "The Work of Sabbath." Check out these essays for other ways to define Sabbath and consider what it could mean in your life.

This is a book about a crusty old practice called Sabbath, but it's really a book about time. Sabbath became the lens through which we saw ourselves: the ways we hurry and the deep goodness in the moments when we don't. Through Sabbath, we came to new understandings about ourselves, our work, our dreams for our children, and the passions that drive us.

Let us begin.

1

Beginnings

If the world were merely seductive, that would be easy. If it were merely challenging, that would be no problem. But I arise in the morning torn between a desire to improve the world and a desire to enjoy the world. This makes it hard to plan the day.

—E. B. White[1]

"Something's got to change."

"I know, but what? How?"

The island was working on us, like it had for thousands who'd traveled here before us.

Back in the sixth century, the legend goes, an Irish monk hopped aboard a boat with no steering system, convinced that God and providence would wash him ashore where he needed to be. That place was Iona, the tiny isle in the Inner Hebrides where Christianity touched Scotland for the first time. Columba (later St. Columba) built an abbey church there. A nunnery came later, and for countless generations, Iona was a mission outpost for western Scotland.

Now, some fourteen hundred years later, Iona is a popular spot for pilgrims and tourists with a spiritual bent. My husband Robert and I had traveled there in 2007 with a group from the church I served as associate pastor. I was there as a spiritual guide and tour director but was needing a little guidance and direction of my own.

Iona is famously described as a thin place—a place where heaven draws very close to earth. (My list of thin places also includes hospital deathbeds, labor and delivery rooms, and U2 concerts.)

The craggy landscape, crumbling Celtic landmarks, and sunshine slanting late into the evening make the place feel heavenly. But it was the silence that did something to me. I'm a city girl, always have been, and never realized how accustomed I was to a basic drone of noise until that noise disappeared. There are precious few mechanical sounds on the island. An occasional car. A distant lawn mower, though these are rare because the wandering sheep do most of the grass-trimming work. A plane, so high we could barely hear it, going from London to Reykjavik perhaps. After several days, the silence had seeped into my bones, making my chest heave from the sheer otherworldly beauty of it. I began to crave the silence that begins in the ears and permeates the whole body. A peace that is not thin but *thick*.

It was a peace that held up a mirror to my not-so-peaceful life back home in the suburbs of Washington, DC. We'd traveled via plane, train, bus, and two ferries to escape, but somehow a gaggle of discontented questions had stowed away in my carryon.

My husband Robert and I had numerous soul-searching conversations on that island. Our lives felt way too full, we realized, with two careers, two young children, and volunteer obligations perpetually tugging at us. Not to mention the countless tasks required to keep the lawn minimally mowed (forget gardening), the bills paid (forget filing), and the clothes cleaned (forget folding and *really* forget ironing). None of these household tasks was all that burdensome, but taken together, they often left us feeling we'd never get on top of it all.

Each morning we would ready the girls for school and daycare. Even as I brushed their teeth I felt the clock ticking and the work tasks piling up. "Hurry up, let's go!" was our default phrase; I feared our daughters would someday etch it on our tombstones. Our tempers were too short, our leisure time too chopped up. And yet our neighborhood was full of kids who were enrolled in way more activities than ours were, leaving us feeling that we were failing at our parental duty to give them every opportunity for enrichment and achievement.

We were still reeling from the news that our third child was on the way, the one we called our bonus baby. We were excited with a side of awe. But the question nagged, "How will we do it all?" Our life felt like a 500-piece jigsaw puzzle with 600 pieces.

During the week at Iona, we hiked around the island as part of the Iona Community's weekly pilgrimage. This pilgrimage included a visit to Marble Quarry, not far from the beach where Columba is said to have made landfall. The rocks there are 2.4 billion years old, some of the oldest rocks in the world. I chose three to take home and listened to them clacking in my pockets for the rest of the hike.

We were here long before you, and we'll be here long after you.

There they were: three smooth pebbles of perspective. We have such a short time on this earth. How did we want to live it? Always busy, working on the next project, chore, or errand? Or with an attitude of unhurried trust and joy?

Our last night on the island, these questions, and the night air, beckoned us outside. We scrambled over a fence, climbed a squat hill, found a couple of large tufts of wild grass to sit on, and had our final State of the Union conversation. The sun was setting, although it was nearly 10 p.m. I imagined the sun still shining brightly in Northern Virginia, where the girls would be having a late afternoon snack. I imagined Caroline's blond hair flowing as she rode her bike—the training wheels would be coming off soon—and Margaret's cocoa-brown eyes as she sucked on three fingers and took in everything her big sister did. I gave silent thanks for my mother, who was taking care of them while we floated in the North Atlantic. I missed them. I owed it to them to come home changed. If they were going to be without their mother for a week, they at least deserved a new-and-improved one.

"Something needs to change, but what?" Robert asked. "We both love our jobs. I think you'd be unhappy staying home full time. I suspect I would be, too."

"Maybe it's where we live," I mused. "Things are so crazy in DC. I don't think it's like that everywhere."

"Yes. There are places in the world where you don't get honked at the nanosecond the light turns green." We laughed. "But what about your mother? It's so wonderful to have family nearby. We wouldn't be able to do things like this if it weren't for her."

Our discussion meandered, aimless. We even considered chucking it all and going to live on a farm in the country. This got us laughing again.

"We know nothing about farming," I said. "It would be like a bad reality show."

"Not to mention that that lifestyle is anything but easy," he replied, his practical side showing as always.

No, there would be no geographical cure.

Out of nowhere I said, "What about Sabbath? What if we took a day off from everything each week? Errands, job, housecleaning, all that stuff." The word "Sabbath" tasted strange in my mouth, but something about it felt right, too.

"Soooo . . .," Robert began slowly. "We feel like there's not enough time to get it all done, and now we're going to have even less time to do it?"

"But that's always going to be the case. Let's turn it around and set aside the time for rest and fun. Remember fun?"

He smiled. I continued.

"Right now we take little moments, but that's only after we've finished everything else. It's like we have to 'earn' it. What if we took a whole day no matter what?"

After some discussion, Robert agreed: "Yeah. Let's do it." Then he added, "It's one of those things that sounds easy, but I think it will be hard. Especially for you."

It was. Especially for me.

*   *   *

"Remember the sabbath day to keep it holy." It's one of the Ten Commandments, but one most folks don't take very seriously. It's the cute commandment. The one we easily dismiss.

Sabbath-keeping seems quaint in the twenty-first century. Most people can admit that it's a nice idea, a lofty, pleasant-sounding but unattainable goal. Even among Jews, for whom Sabbath is a key part of religious practice, the sabbath day is relatively rare; a quick Google search turns up surveys suggesting that only a quarter to a third of Jewish households observe the Sabbath in some way. Sabbath feels like one of those cultural trappings from the Bible that doesn't apply any more, like polygamy or washing a guest's feet when they enter a house.

But what's not to like? A day each week without work . . . a day to unplug, unwind, laugh, play, and love. It was worth a try. On one day, we would not multitask. We would not map out the optimal way to get our errands done with cranky kids in tow. We would not shop. We would not plan. We would stop, which is the literal meaning of Sabbath–"Shabbat" in Hebrew. We would rest, and we would not expend energy except to do the things that we enjoy.

The world would go on without us. We would be dispensable. We would let God's grace seep into us in a way that it can't when our lives are crammed full of activity.

For one day a week, we would let the laundry sit in the basket, let the leaves languish on the lawn, let the bills sit unpaid on the desk.

For one day a week, we would take a day of rest that, we hoped, would help put the remainder of the week in better perspective.

But how, *how* were we going make this happen? How does it work, with two careers and three children, and the relentless tasks that make up life in the modern world? As a pastor, I work every Sunday morning, plus many Sunday afternoons. There are committee meetings in the evenings, Saturday retreats, and late-night phone calls with parishioners in need. Weekends are our time to catch up on chores and errands.

The laundry will not do itself. If we didn't have small kids in the house, we could put off going to the grocery store, gamely subsisting on whatever we might find in our kitchen. But it feels irresponsible to feed growing bodies a meal consisting of Wheaties, half a bag of frozen pearl onions, and Catalina dressing.

There had to be some best practices—after all, people have been doing this for thousands of years. In my post-Iona glow, I decided to consult some experts, hopeful that they could help with the "how." I found every book on Sabbath I could get my hands on. These were helpful companions, as far as they went. Other people apparently also found the pace of life as confounding as I did. Other people saw our 24-7 world to be exhausting and dysfunctional too.

The problem was, parenting is a 24-7 job. Parenting *is* work. And none of the books I found had much to say about how to do Sabbath with children. They were beautiful books with urgent pleas to take a break, to observe a holy rhythm of work and rest. But they seemed to be written by people without children, or folks whose kids were grown.

The Jewish-oriented books were fascinating, and the rituals were beautiful. *This is deep stuff,* I mused, as I read about candles and fresh challah bread, prayers said by mother and father, and the blessing of children. These books were more family oriented and at least acknowledged the presence of children more than the Christian books did. I read about homes in which children tear toilet paper the day before Sabbath for the family's use; tearing is one of the activities that's prohibited on Shabbat.

But the orthodox Sabbath did not suit us. A stay-at-home mother seemed to be a key ingredient to making it all work. One book dispatched with the arrangements for Shabbat in a single sentence: "Preparations intensify on Friday as we engage in shopping, cooking, and cleaning to make everything ready for Shabbat."[2] I was incredulous: *That's it?!?* How exactly does the challah get purchased? The house tidied? The food prepared? Who remembers to unscrew the light in the refrigerator so it won't come on the next day? (Thou shalt not kindle fire.) How does all this happen before sundown—or more precisely, eighteen minutes before sundown as the rabbis specified?

Other books were more practical, with step-by-step guides, recipes, and cheerful urges to do what you can and start where you are. One author, a working mother herself, provided a charmingly frenzied diary of her preparations for Shabbat, including a tense countdown to the candle-lighting moment.[3] Another writer titled her essay "Preparing for Shabbat: A Frantic Approach."[4]

Ultimately, we couldn't go the Orthodox Jewish route. We are Christians. Copying the Jewish Shabbat felt like co-opting a practice that was not our own.

We decided to set the books on a shelf for possible reference and figure it out ourselves.

For a couple of years after Iona, we dabbled with Sabbath. We'd get it right one weekend and miss the next four. We'd high-five ourselves for going two weeks in a row, then find ourselves three months later, worn out and dazed, and one of us would ask, "Whatever happened to the Sabbath thing?"

Oh, yeah. That.

Meanwhile, James was born. He's almost three now, our only boy, who inherited Matchbox cars from family friends and will turn anything—potato masher, toilet paper tube—into a pretend vehicle. Margaret is four, our exuberant child who never walks when she can skip and who cycles through a dozen or more moods each day.

Caroline is nearly eight, an age at which she is starting to expand her world, yet still likes being around us. She reads Magic Tree House books, devouring them in forty-five-minute bursts, sneaking them under the dinner table. She's involved in a few after-school activities—mainly Girl Scouts and piano lessons—and when we talk to friends with older children about how we don't want to overcommit her, they look at us sympathetically, as if they want to pat our hands and say, "Good luck with that."

*　*　*

In the months after Iona and James's birth, we muddled along with our fitful Sabbath observance, doing well, then falling off the wagon. Then something happened that helped crystallize things and got us serious about Sabbath again.

Caroline's elementary school made some changes to the bus route that delayed the kids' arrival home in the afternoon. Many parents found this unacceptable and decided to mount a petition and letter-writing campaign. After three weeks of phone calls, letters, and updates at the bus stop, the schedule got changed: other children would stay on the bus longer so that our kids would get home four minutes sooner.

Four whole minutes.

The parental blitzkrieg for the sake of four minutes of afternoon time struck me as ridiculous. When the draft petition went out over e-mail, I wrote a painstaking response, picking my words as carefully as a SWAT team member diffusing a bomb.

The fact that the whole affair bothered me so much was a sign, I felt. I didn't want to live the kind of life in which an extra four minutes were so crucial to my family's schedule that I would petition the county government to get my way.

But the bus stop petition exposed the insanity in my own life. I, too, treated time as a scarce commodity to be hoarded. It was a constant struggle to keep from gripping tightly to every four-minute nugget of time, maximizing every moment, multitasking as if my life depended on it.

I'm no saint when it comes to time. I do not smile beatifically at the grocery store checker with the crashed register. I do not breathe deep cleansing breaths at life's little annoyances. One afternoon on my way to a meeting, I made a wrong turn onto a street that—of course—had several blocks of stop-and-go traffic to suffer through before I found a place to turn around. Did I accept this situation with the Zen-like equanimity of a woman who refuses to sign a bus stop petition? No, I pounded the steering wheel and shrieked with frustration.

I work more than I should and find it hard to rest—surely I will let someone down if I take time off. I find every excuse to put off silence, meditation, and prayer, even as I preach about their importance to the congregation I serve. I'm way too plugged into technology for too many hours of the day.

I feel muddled by my own spiritual contradictions. I want my children to live an unhurried childhood, even as I jam tiny feet into shoes, scooting us out the door so we won't be late. I believe that our constant drive for kids to *Go! Do! Be!* can have perilous consequences. But as Caroline brings home flyers and permission slips for science club, campouts, and Spanish, I see how overloading one's children is such a gradual process—a thousand small, well-intentioned decisions, not a single cataclysmic blunder.

So after too many fits and starts, we're going all in: one year of Sabbath practice. That's one day, every week, from September to August. There will be no work. No tidying. No answering e-mails. No sermon writing. Those errands and chores that take up a weekend? They will have to be done on the nonsabbath day, shoehorned into the weekdays, or (gulp) not done at all.

Could we pull it off?

We were about to find out.

* * *

Christians typically get an understanding of Sabbath from the Ten Commandments and from the story of creation. According to Genesis 1, God made the universe and everything in it and then rested for a time: "On the seventh day God finished the work that he had done, and he rested on the seventh day from all the work that he had done. So God blessed the seventh day and hallowed it, because on it God rested from all the work that he had done in creation" (Gen. 2:2–3). God did it, so we should do it. The rhythm is established.

But for Jews, there is another narrative that resonates as strongly as the creation story. The sabbath day is a gift for the Jewish people because it reminds them of the time when their people were slaves in Egypt, captive to Pharaoh's regime. They were forced to work, not six days a week but every day of the week (Ex. 1). There was no freedom, no relief—just the constant lashing of expectations: do more, produce more, build more.

But God brought the people out of slavery. God parted the Red Sea and gave them safe passage to freedom, and with it, the Ten Commandments. Among them? *For six days shall work be done, but the seventh day is a Sabbath of solemn rest* (Ex. 20:8–11). So the Jewish observance of Sabbath is an exclamation to the world:

We are not slaves to the empire anymore!
  We are free!

I'm a captive too, but of a very different sort. I feel enslaved to the type-A madness of my environment and my own soul.

I'm longing for the Promised Land.

And Sabbath is my Red Sea, I'm sure of it.

2

September

*A Buddhist monk visiting New York was told by his Western host
that they could save ten minutes by making a complex transfer in
the subway at Grand Central Station. When they emerged from
the underground in Central Park, the monk sat down on a bench.
His host wanted to know what he was doing. "I thought we should
enjoy the ten minutes," the monk replied.[1]*

Sabbath isn't easy for anyone—there's a reason few people take
it on—but our family has some particular challenges. I am in my
first year of a new job as solo pastor of a small congregation. As an
associate pastor on a large staff for six years, there were other people
on call during my days off, and I covered for them in turn. Now the
buck stops with me. Meetings will be scheduled, emergency surger-
ies will take place, and people will need me during the time I have
designated as Sabbath.

Robert is an information technology professional in a growing
company that can't hire people fast enough to keep up with the work.
During the week he usually leaves for the office before our children
are even awake. After the kids are in bed at night, he's back on the
computer. Weekends are for haircuts, bill paying, and yard work.

As a second grader, Caroline's after-school and weekend activities are starting to ramp up, and I know things will only get more
challenging the older she gets. On the upside, Margaret and James,
who aren't in school yet, seem to have an unhurried Sabbath mental-
ity wired into their small bodies:

"Can we color together?" (Who cares if it's 8:20 on a Monday
morning?)

"Will you set up my train tracks?" (The fact that the farmers' market closes in thirty minutes is completely irrelevant.)

The two of them will be glad for a one-day reprieve from having to tag along on errands. So will Caroline, actually—she's a homebody at heart. But Sabbath is more than a day; it's a mind-set. And in all our Sabbath dabbling the last few years, I rarely got into that mind-set, given the constant low-level vigilance required with small children. The younger ones need us to run interference so an older kid doesn't clobber them. Toddler bottoms must be wiped. Children get thirsty and need a drink of water.

*   *   *

The first and most important decision is, when will our sabbath day be? If we choose Sunday, we only get half a day of rest, since Sunday morning is work time for me at the church. This makes Saturday my first choice—it gives us a whole day of rest, and it's appealing to be able to sleep in. ("Sleep in" now means 7 a.m., if we're lucky.)

Robert, whose parents are pastors, says, "I don't know . . . Sunday downtime is kinda in my DNA. My dad *always* took a nap Sunday afternoon. We'd watch football or lie around. Besides, I'm not sure we can pull off a Saturday Sabbath. That would mean that Sunday afternoon is the only time for us to get weekend stuff done. That's not a lot of time."

I counter, "Yes, but if we choose Sunday, then we're not really getting a full day. And that's what we say we need. I don't think Sunday afternoon is enough."

After a lot of back and forth, we decide to try Saturday. But we're not sure how strict to be. What if one of us has to work that day? Will we say no to stuff rather than compromise our commitment to Sabbath?

"This isn't a stunt," I tell Robert. "I'm not out to get myself fired because I refuse to do my job on Saturday. That's not what this is about. I feel like we need to be flexible or this won't work. We'll move the Sabbath when we have to. But we'll *move* it, not let it go."

We are fortunate that our religious tradition is not strict about a specific day. Sure, Sunday is the "Lord's Day," and almost all Christians recognize that day as the Sabbath. But not all. Some, like Seventh-Day Adventists, take a Saturday Sabbath. However, most

Christians we know don't take a Sabbath at all—anything we choose would be a step up. Jesus certainly wasn't strict about the Sabbath; he violated it all the time for worthwhile things. Many modern Sabbath practitioners invite people to be flexible and take Sabbath when it makes most sense for them.

So we have the freedom to decide what works for us. But will flexibility disrupt the rhythm? Will a floating Sabbath make things too confusing? And what kind of spiritual statement is that? "God, we trust you to provide what we need, and we want to put this practice at the center of our lives. So we'll be penciling you in when it's optimal for us."

As it stands now, it often takes me half a sabbath day to unwind and let go of the worries over things I should be doing. Will I ever really get into the practice? Will I grow to resent this time of enforced rest and relaxation as I fall further behind? It seems unlikely, but I have no idea. Maybe there are people who don't like to slow down.

And what will the kids think? Will our kids grow up to hate the Sabbath? I know folks of a certain generation who remember Sabbath as a dour and humorless time. Only religious activities were allowed, like Bible-themed board games or devotional reading. That's not our approach . . . although we've been thinking that Sabbath wouldn't involve a lot of television or video games. Being zoned out in front of the television doesn't seem very Sabbath-y. But curtailing screen time is something the kids will protest.

People wish there were more hours in the day—I've wished that—and now we are effectively reducing our week from 168 hours to 144. Underneath my excitement is a low-grade desperation. We're handicapping ourselves, effectively tying one day behind our backs. Will it be worth it? Or will it make the rest of our days that much more hectic? Will our house, our yard, our lives fall into a state of ever-encroaching dishevelment?

*   *   *

The next thing to work out is "what." What is work? What should we be ceasing from?

We have a child who's barely out of diapers. Our daughters are only self-entertaining for periodic bursts—certainly not for a whole day. There's a basic level of upkeep involved in everyday living.

While caring for family is a joy, it's also work. And if we're already doing *that* kind of work, it's easy to picture ourselves lurching, zombie-like, into other kinds of work without even realizing it. Caring for kids becomes the gateway drug to more tasks. *If you're going to do that, you might as well do this too . . .*

Another gray area: I am a hopeless "Cleaner-as-I-Go." If I'm walking upstairs and I see a pair of shoes that need to be taken up, what do I do? Does it undermine the restful, leave-it-be mind-set to pick them up and take them with me? What if it's a ten-pound laundry basket instead of a pair of shoes? Does it matter? If I don't do it and it continues to poke at me, is that a distraction to be managed, or do I complete the task, because, hey, I have the freedom to define this as I please?

And what about food? Cooking is work, and mealtimes are a big chore around here right now. Until recently, James couldn't have peanut butter. Meanwhile, Caroline loves it and Margaret likes it only sometimes. Before I had kids, I swore I wouldn't be a short-order cook, but they've gotta eat. It's not unusual for Robert or me to finish making the kids lunch, plunk into a chair, and think, "Oh geez, I have to eat *too?*"

I mention this to Robert, who hits upon a brilliant solution. Sabbath lunch will be Bagel Bites and fruit: not quite the roast chicken and kugel that make up traditional Shabbat feasts, but they're easy, and everyone in our house likes them. Problem solved.

As for dinner, we decide to cook together on Saturday night. "That way it'll be something we do together," Robert says.

"Yes, just like the olden days," I muse, remembering our early married life when we would spend a couple of hours each evening figuring out a recipe, tag-teaming each other as sous chef. We never had to worry about how long it took.

All these decisions have my mind spinning. I find myself envying the orthodox Jewish way, in which the boundaries have been worked out. There are thirty-nine categories of work that are prohibited on the Sabbath, everything from cooking to tying knots to kindling fire.[2] Jewish folk have recipes to prepare, prayers to say, services to attend, songs to sing. Christian Sabbath observance has been robust in its own way through the centuries but without the deep rituals that provide color and texture to the experience.

To be fair, there are modern Jews who find these rituals to be cumbersome and prohibitive to an observance of Sabbath. But at least the communal knowledge is there. I feel like we're on our own, setting our own boundaries. Being able to do things our way should feel freeing, but part of me would like to have someone simply tell us what to do, even if the prohibitions seem odd or silly.

One writer takes on the practice of pretearing the toilet paper in this way:

> Preparing paper in advance seems so remote from holy time. The objective outsider might say, "This is pure legalism and highly ridiculous besides; there's no work involved in tearing a piece of perforated toilet paper on the Sabbath." To which an insider might respond, "Look how clever the Rabbis were: even in as mundane a place as the bathroom, one is reminded of the uniqueness of the day."[3]

I may be a Sabbath outsider and insider—I can relate to both perspectives.

The Work of Sabbath: Don't Go Changing

I tell a friend about our upcoming Sabbath project and our attempts to figure out what's allowed on that day, and she suggests this definition of work: any activity that changes one's environment. So Sabbath would be a day of giving up trying to change things.

What this means is not trying to improve oneself: no progress on the clutter or headway on the to-do list. I begin to imagine it: the petrified cat puke on the floor, the dried strand of spaghetti snaked on the table, and the e-mail marked "urgent," whether or not it really is. These things would remain unswiffered, unwiped, and unacknowledged.

I shudder, but I reluctantly decide that not changing things seems like a good place to start.

Sabbath is a day of trusting that, as my mother likes to say, "Everything everywhere is all right already." And if it isn't all right, to let it be not-all-right. Sometimes the way things *get* all right is by our not mucking with them.

I once read that Alfred Hitchcock had a novel approach when his actors would get stuck on a scene. Hitchcock would come in and start clowning around to lift the tension. Invariably the actors would have a breakthrough and get back on track. Later, Hitchcock would explain his tactic by saying, "You were pushing. It never comes through pushing."[4]

I realize how much of my life is about pushing things to happen. I am the manager of the household. Part of this is temperament, and part of it is circumstance: I work part time and have the space in my life to schedule appointments, oversee homework, and run the preschool carpool. But even I need reminders that I am not indispensable.

Several years ago, as part of ministry training, I spent a summer as a hospital chaplain. I knew it would be a challenging summer but was excited about the opportunity. My supervisor and I set a whole slew of learning goals. After the first day of hospital rounds, I came home exhausted and cranky. Something wasn't right. Robert and I had been trying to get pregnant, and I took a test that night. Sure enough: positive.

My well-crafted learning goals evaporated. Now the goal was to survive by shoving saltines into my mouth between calls, sleeping during the overnight shifts, and learning which meals in the cafeteria would keep the nausea at bay. I probably learned as much as I would have with my overly earnest goals, but I was along for the ride instead of driving the experience.

Illness, pregnancy, caregiving, a death in the family—all these are a reminder of the mystery of life that is bigger than ourselves. People sometimes say, "It's a shame that it took a tragedy for me figure out what's important." I wonder if Sabbath can be that reminder for us, every single week, under more mundane circumstances. Perhaps if we let things go for one day and give up trying to change everything for the better, it will help us see that things are pretty OK right now.

*   *   *

We decide to start our year of Sabbath in September. As parents, our lives still conform to the academic year.

Unfortunately, Labor Day weekend comes and goes without a Sabbath.

There is no conversation, no deliberate decision. We work all weekend, getting the kids ready for school, buying the last-minute items Caroline needs for second grade. We dig out the backpack from the closet where it's been buried since June. We open the lunch box after a summer in the kitchen cabinet, hoping it isn't fuzzy on the inside thanks to a forgotten apple core or crust of bread.

We take some time for fun, enjoying the pool on the last weekend before it closes for the season. But it's not a leisurely sort of fun. It's the recreation that comes tinged with guilt and a nagging sense that there's still more to do.

Monday night I get into bed and sigh, "Guess we missed it again."

Robert deadpans, "It's right there in the name: *Labor* Day. We were doomed from the start."

We realize how easy it is to become unmindful, to just do what's next. A body at motion will stay in motion: go to work, come home, make dinner, eat, get the kids to bed, clean up the kitchen, tidy the family room, answer e-mails, fall into bed. Lather, rinse, repeat.

The first few days of school are filled with forms, sign-ups, and meetings with teachers. The kids have a hard time getting back into the groove. There are tears, fights in the morning, and covers pulled over the head when I flip on the light. I dread the teenage years if I'm already having to peel them out of bed.

* * *

The following weekend, things go a little better. It is an improvement over Labor Day weekend because we make a conscious decision to have Sabbath. But that feels like the only improvement.

The weekend is not without its fun. On Friday night, Robert and I go to a play while the kids sleep over at my mother's apartment downtown. Saturday morning, Robert picks up the kids while I finish my sermon for Sunday. (Clearly I need to find a way to finish writing sermons before Saturday.) Our family Sabbath begins around noon with the kids bursting into the house.

Caroline rushes to give me a hug and holds up a bag of candy from her MaDear. "Can we have some right now?"

Robert says, "No, it's lunchtime."

Margaret chimes in: "Can we eat in the basement? I want to watch Electric Company!"

This is typical. Our children usually come home from my mother's house hung over from television and sweets and begging us for more of the same. The whining continues for the rest of the afternoon.

I'd had an image of what Sabbath would be like. I'd expected a hush over the house as each person drifted from one self-directed activity to the next. Maybe a trio would form for a board game while the other two read. Then one would peel off and ask to color with one of the readers. It would be a dance of quiet activity, together and apart. That's the way Sabbath is written about, in my experience. The book covers feature a scripty font and a peaceful landscape, not sticky fingers and needling requests. *Those smarty-pants writers should see us now,* I think with a sharp laugh to myself.

We aren't parents that plan our kids' every move. But our kids need some direction from us. They are bored and tired. They can't think of anything to do. Skirmishes and petty complaints flare up throughout the day. There is yelling and the slamming of doors.

That night we have a relic on the calendar from before our Sabbath experiment began, a concert to raise money to rebuild a children's home in Haiti that had been devastated by the earthquake. I think the girls will enjoy it, but it adds another layer of un-Sabbathness to the day. I know that the afternoon will end abruptly with a tumble of commands: "Finish up your dinner, there won't be food there. Go to the bathroom. Put on your shoes. You need a sweater."

The imperative voice is very anti-Sabbath, I think.

But the concert is wonderful, and for the first time all day, we are relaxed and in the moment. The performers tell stories about life in Haiti through dance and drumming. The music is visceral, emotional. I feel chastened that I, in all my abundance, can be so pinched and anxious.

On the way home I receive a text from Robert that he and James had a fun evening too, and that James fell asleep after only one story at bedtime.

Later that night, I say, "Are we insane for trying this?"

Robert jokes, "Maybe those people who enroll their kids in back-to-back activities have the right idea."

I laugh, then pause a moment. "Remember when I had that oral surgery a few years back? They told me to take the pain medication on time, not to wait until I started feeling uncomfortable."

"To stay ahead of the pain."

"Exactly. Our day was like that."

"Like oral surgery?"

"Heh . . . yeah. No, I mean we couldn't ever stay ahead of things. We had no plan. The kids needed this and that, then they'd fight, and we were tired too, so it kinda failed."

"Is Sabbath something that just happens . . . or is it something that we have to make happen?"

"I think with kids it's the latter."

*   *   *

The next Sabbath dawns bright and sunny. Fall in Virginia is a long and brilliant season, a luxurious gift after growing up in Texas. (My uncle, who lives in Dallas, likes to say, "Fall is pretty in Texas. It's usually on a Thursday.") It seems like an opportunity to be seized. The kids' stir-craziness from last week leaps into my mind and I look at Robert, who is thinking the same thing.

"Let's go somewhere."

After a quick Google to find out what's happening in the area (*Is Googling cheating?* I wonder), we end up at the International Children's Festival at Wolf Trap Park.

Outings are a double-edged sword on the Sabbath, we learn. If you're away from home, you can't be tempted by the pile of clean laundry in the basket, creased with wrinkles, or by the sheaf of papers beckoning to be filed. But leaving the house with little ones requires effort, an assembly line of potty and shoes and a snack for good measure. We pack a simple picnic lunch and get everyone into the car and buckled, and Robert turns the ignition.

Gas light.

No big deal. We stop for gas. Robert makes faces at the kids through the window as he fuels up. As he gets back in the car he pauses. "Do you have any cash? I'm not sure I have enough. We'd better run to the ATM over there."

I quip, "OK, but it's pretty much feeling like a Saturday now. Why don't we head back home for the cardboard recycling? Maybe whip up a grocery list?"

Once at the festival, we sit on the grass listening to a Celtic band while a group of African drummers warms up nearby. James is eating his turkey sandwich with the all-the-time-in-the-world relish of a toddler. Meanwhile I am poring over the schedule.

"There's a puppet show, and a drama troupe, and oh! Dancers from Peru! But it's all clear across the park. And it all starts in ten minutes. We'll never make it!"

Robert looks at me.

Oh, right.

Once we start walking around, things relax. We see the Peruvian troupe with children and adults dancing together in traditional costume. Caroline and Margaret get their faces painted while James looks on, then Robert and I help them sample the instruments provided by a local youth orchestra.

While waiting in line for popsicles, a smiling volunteer asks if I wouldn't mind completing a survey about the festival. Before I can stop myself, I say, "Thank you, but no."

I blink, checking myself. Where did that come from? I've done survey work and even knocked on doors for political campaigns, so I know how excruciating it can be to put oneself out there. I always say yes to such folks, especially volunteers.

Then I remember that our work on Sabbath is to avoid changing things. Maybe registering one's opinion, even in this small way, counts as effecting change. One of the nasty lies that Sabbath confronts is the myth of indispensability, the idea that the world needs me in order to keep functioning. It's very flattering to be asked one's opinion. But I can easily let this one go.

We learn that family outings will work as a sabbath activity but perhaps not ones that have things starting at specific times. It's hard for me to let go of the schedule, wondering what we're missing somewhere else. I'm a constant and gifted planner, and having multiple stages to choose from is too much on a Sabbath. It would be like holding a compulsive shoppers' support group at an outlet mall. On Black Friday.

In the big scheme of things, being on time to a puppet show is not on a level with being on time to school each morning. On the other hand, if it's truly a day of rest, why should clocks be a consideration at all? Sabbath is a time when we need a break from the clock. Maybe that's what Rabbi Abraham Joshua Heschel meant when he called the Sabbath a "palace in time."[5]

Our day ends with Bob McGrath—that's Bob from *Sesame Street*—who emcees the closing ceremony. We learn from the introduction that he is almost eighty years old, though he's so energetic I have a hard time believing it. At the end of the performance, he leads the crowd in "Sing."

"Sing . . . sing a song, sing out loud, sing out strong."

The whole crowd joins in. The five of us are sitting down front, the younger two on laps with Caroline sitting quietly nearby, watching Bob's every move. With each chorus, another group comes from backstage. Young people from Estonia and Jamaica and Switzerland appear. All are singing along.

"Don't worry that it's not good enough for anyone else to hear. Just sing . . . sing a song."

It feels like our yearlong sabbath experiment is finally under way. And maybe it's OK if it isn't good enough. Maybe it's OK just to sing.

*   *   *

"You guys go on without me—really," I say, "I'll catch up with you after my meeting."

"Are you sure?" Robert asks. "We could wait and all have Sabbath together on Sunday."

"No, I'll catch up with you somehow."

It's only three weeks into the sabbath year and already we have a Sabbath that conflicts with a Saturday church event—a meeting of the Presbyterian ministers and elders in this area. I am expected to be there. All throughout the meeting I find myself wondering what the family is up to. Knowing that they're together, enjoying one another, gives me a boost of sabbath energy, even though I'm on the clock.

I drive home, eager to hear about their morning.

"It was so cool!" Caroline gushes. "The guy was like a comedian and magician for kids, and he did silly stuff like put a diaper on his head."

"Then we goed to a carnival!" James pipes up.

"It was in the parking lot of the mall," Margaret explains. "We got funnel cake."

"Sounds great," I say. We spend the rest of the afternoon puttering around the house, and miraculously, there is no squabbling.

Later, when I tell a friend about these September Sabbath experiences, she asks, "So how is Sabbath time different from family time? Because what you're describing sounds a lot like family time to me."

It's a good question. Lots of people spend time together as a family and are intentional about setting aside that time, if not weekly, then regularly. It would be presumptuous—and a little ridiculous—for me to barrel in and say, "No, you're doing it wrong! Family time isn't enough. You really need to be doing Sabbath-keeping! Here, light a candle."

But what's behind this impulse for Sabbath? Is this about family bonding, or is there something deeper going on?

I think back to my week with Robert on Iona so many years ago. A family of five was also there at the time. They'd been living there for the better part of a year.

One day, I was walking from the nunnery ruins back to the abbey and saw the kids walking about twenty feet ahead of me. They were completely unhurried. One of the girls suddenly flung an arm over her sister's shoulder. The move was loving, casual, and completely carefree. It felt like a quintessential gesture of childhood. *We have all the time in the world.*

I've seen my children amble in that same way. Our harried, two-career existence cannot take that away from them. Not even my jarring entreaties to "put your shoes on NOW" will knock it out of them. It is part of them, a beautiful dimension of childhood. But someday they'll be adults with places to go and people to see. What kind of adults will they be? Hurried and harried?

So yes, Sabbath is a way of modeling a different relationship with time, one that values relationship over achievement. But it's more than a parenting technique.

It's been said that our checkbooks are spiritual documents. How we budget and spend our money demonstrates what we believe and hold dear. Do we give a portion away? Do we spend it on trendy clothes and trinkets? Our money reveals who we are and what we believe about the world and about God.

But our calendars are spiritual documents, too. To-do lists and Google Calendars are statements of faith. Our statement of faith said, "We are busy with good and important things but have no time to stop and enjoy God's creation. We believe in our own self-importance. We believe in our need to keep up appearances of having it all together. We believe that we are in control of our own lives." We would never have said such things aloud. But our lives betrayed us, screaming way louder than our demure affirmations about the Holy.

So a weekly Sabbath provides some intentionality to our life together. Sabbath puts the focus on God and God's gracious invitation to rest from one's work. That's what distinguishes it from family time.

Sabbath Hack: Coin a New Term

For folks living the hurried life, Sabbath doesn't come naturally. It feels weird, like writing with the wrong hand. The things that need to be done start to nag. It's easy to get ticked off—maybe a tiny bit panicked: *All this stuff is piling up; tomorrow will be payback time when we have to play catch-up. What's the use?*

I'm worried that my mind-set will short-circuit Sabbath every time. I need a solution—something that will tame the hamster wheel in my brain. My husband is a former computer programmer, and I like the idea of a "hack": a trick that isn't pretty but works. My first Sabbath hack is to create a new word:

Sabbathly.
Sabbath-ly.
Adverb.
To do something *in the manner of* Sabbath.

There are times when I don't feel restful. I don't feel the joy of the moment. I don't feel connected to God. But I believe that we can act our way into a new feeling. We can look at life, with its imperfections and annoyances, and change it for the better by acting as if it's already better. We can let our language guide us. Words do more than describe our reality; they also shape it. I need a new word: Sabbathly.

Fortunately, "Sabbathly" can happen any time, not only on the Sabbath.

I can act as if the kids and I have all the time in the world in the mornings before school. That doesn't mean that we do, but it means that I am a different person. I do things Sabbathly. I still have to cajole, remind, even put hands on shoulders and steer a day-dreaming child toward the sink to spit the toothpaste. But becoming Banshee Mother doesn't help anyone, and it doesn't seem to get us out of the house any faster, either.

I can act like the relaxed person I all-too-rarely am, and then over time, maybe I become her.

During the week, we can do our work Sabbathly: feeling the warm water on our hands as we do the dishes, driving the speed limit, pushing the mower over the lawn, completely *there*. We can go at the pace required for the work: not too fast, not too slow.

We can be with people Sabbathly: looking them in the eyes, not over their shoulder or down at our smart phones; laughing with them; acting as if we have all the time in the world, even if we don't.

We can observe the Sabbath Sabbathly: making the decision that even if the work is pulling at us, we are going to focus our attention elsewhere. We can act ourselves into a different way of being.

And we can notice the times that we are living Sabbathly and un-Sabbathly. We can be in the midst of a major home project, with its multiple unforeseen trips to the hardware store, and be doing it Sabbathly, with joy and mindfulness. Or we can be sipping a cup of tea with a book open on our lap un-Sabbathly, with fretful distraction.

On the surface, it seems like a fakey thing to do. I'm not a fan of pretending. But living Sabbathly doesn't feel like pretending. Instead it feels like an act of hope. Sabbathly says, "I am a big, frantic, con-flicted mess. But I am going to breathe, smile, and laugh. I am going to demonstrate my willingness to be peaceful. And that's a start."

That's all we can do, is start. And start again.

3

October

Six days shall you be a workaholic;
on the seventh day, shall you join the serene company of
   human beings.

Six days shall you take orders from your boss;
on the seventh day, shall you be master/mistress of your own
   life.

Six days shall you toil in the market;
on the seventh day, shall you detach from money matters.

Six days shall you create, drive, create, invent, push;
on the seventh day, shall you reflect.

Six days shall you be the perfect success;
on the seventh day, shall you remember that not everything is
   in your power.

Six days shall you be a miserable failure;
on the seventh day, shall you be on top of the world.

Six days shall you enjoy the blessings of work;
on the seventh day, shall you understand that being is as
   important as doing.

—Blu Greenberg[1]

I know parents who create a sense of adventure for their kids, whose homes are a constant happy jumble of homemade treats and crafts. Some efforts are successful and some aren't, but that's part of the fun. There are construction projects sprawled in the garage and wild wrestling matches in the family room. These homes have carpets with crayon shavings ground into them and tablecloths crusted with Play-Doh, but it all somehow works as hip parent decor. I know parents who manage to avoid the mundane consistencies of an early bedtime or a designated place for homework, yet their kids thrive. Childhood is a grand boisterous time.

I envy those zany parents. We are not that.

I am very organized. Robert would say, pathologically so. I have a very low threshold for clutter. When I reach the breaking point, I burst into a grumbling flurry of cleaning and tidying, a creature Robert calls the White Tornado. I don't cry over spilled milk, but when the puddle spreads over a tablecloth that emerged from the basket of clean laundry only an hour before, my face darkens in spite of myself. When I'm in the middle of a thought or a task, I find it way too easy to answer a kid's request for attention with "Just a few more minutes, sweetie. Why don't you go watch something until I'm done?"

We love our kids fiercely. We play with them and do the occasional weird art project. It's just that we're not wild-and-crazy folks by nature. Our kids are bright and engaged with the world, but they are not rowdy and kinesthetic. They are a little nerdy, like their parents. They have to be pulled away from books in order to come to dinner. Their mischief consists of taking an entire pad of sticky notes and labeling items in our house. (Microwave: "Hot!" My bedroom door: "Pastor's Room, Do Not Enter.") They are not the crawling-out-on-the-roof type, like the exuberant first grader of a friend of mine.

So we're not zany parents. But I've learned over the years to embrace what we do provide—after the White Tornado has subsided, that is: a peaceful place. Thoughtful questions and a sense of ritual. A bit of calm and order. A place for things, so that when Caroline wants to write a letter to her grandparents, I can hand her the basket with envelopes and stamps. There are nooks for reading, comfortable places to snuggle, and a designated room where kids and adults can go to chill out. A calming sense of structure. Strength and home.

This isn't the only way to be, and certainly not the best way to be. But it's the way Robert and I know how to be, given our personalities and those of our children, and the fact that there are three of them and both of us work outside the home. Our lives can only tolerate so much unraveling before major things start falling through the cracks. Zaniness becomes a hassle if you can't find the permission slip on the morning of the field trip.

But staying on top of things is exhausting.

This is why Sabbath is becoming important to our family. On one day a week, I don't need to be organized, to keep things running like a Swiss watch. Robert doesn't need to consider the most efficient way to get the errands done. On one day, we simply get to be . . . and maybe engage in a monster tickle fight with our kids. And in doing so, we make a statement of faith: the tickle fight is as vital as our work is—perhaps even more so.

I am not complaining about the tasks of parenthood. I am noting a truth: even if you're not a creature of habit like I am, a lot of parenting is painfully repetitive. I've heard that the average baby uses 6,000 diapers before becoming toilet trained. I ponder our family's 18,000 diapers—I wonder how much landfill space that entails—and I think about how much time Robert and I have spent diapering these last few years.

I vary the lunches I make for Caroline, not because she wants variety—she doesn't—but because making peanut butter sandwiches for 180 days in a row, every year, might cause a repetitive stress injury in my brain.

We don't like to admit to the monotony, especially if we know someone who'd give anything to have children; or someone whose child is sick; or someone who has lost a child to illness, accident, or other tragedy. I know all of the above.

But it's true. Parenthood contains moments of bewilderment and joy, but it can also be deadly dull, punctuated by spilled juice and kid-on-kid hitting. Sabbath doesn't save us from the dullness, but it does provide a set-apart time—an opportunity to reconnect with the idea of parenting as a holy vocation, even when life seems an unholy mess.

When I was pregnant with Caroline, a friend who'd given birth a few months prior said, "I never knew how much my parents loved me until I had my baby." As she held her infant daughter and rubbed her fuzzy blond head, I thought about my friend's newfound wisdom, the realization of the awesome responsibility of parenthood, and the flood of unconditional love that had apparently come to her.

Then I had Caroline, who liked to nurse around the clock, whose hungry cry of "aaa-AAAA!!" bore into me like a screwdriver to the skull.

After dealing with a bout of infant gastroenteritis, including several days of diapers that could have been designated as Superfund sites, I talked to my friend again: "You remember what you said about realizing how much your parents loved you?"

"Yes."

"Was that, like, a fuzzy romantic kind of idea? Or was it that you finally realized how much work parenting is and were amazed at the fact that your parents did it for you?"

"Are you kidding? The second one!"

"Yeah. I didn't get that until now."

I feel fortunate that our children are basically content and in good health. The days run together, but they revolve around getting dressed and putting on shoes, not administering medication or visiting specialists. Still, a person craves novelty. There's novelty in parenting, but it's embedded in a year-in, year-out slow march of days.

"You're thinking about this all wrong," says a friend and mother of two. "Parenthood isn't repetitive. It's liturgical."

I laugh, "You *would* say that; you're an Episcopalian. Everything's liturgical to you guys." But I know what she means. What we do is sacred work. The fact that it's repeated doesn't make it devalued. The work provides stability and comfort. And it makes the deviation from the routine that much more delicious.

Sabbath ensures that one day out of seven, there is a disruption in the liturgy, a break in the rhythm. There is no table set the night before with cereal bowls, because maybe we won't have cereal for breakfast. On Sabbath, there's no reason to choose the fastest option. We can eat what our bellies tell us to eat, whatever the random ingredients we find in the kitchen make possible. Coffee cake? Waffles? (One Jewish writer allows his children to eat sugary cereals on the Sabbath, a sweet indulgence that's off limits on other days.[2])

Taking a break from the routine changes the way I think about the routine.

*   *   *

The fall is still beckoning us outside, so we're doing Sabbath out and about. The cabin fever days will come soon enough, so we get out of the house as much as possible. In October we visit Cox Farms, a pumpkin patch with a kids' carnival atmosphere. There are slides, a hayride, stacks of apples, farm animals, and big plastic bags of fresh, warm kettle corn.

We have gone to Cox Farms every year since Caroline was small. The trip has become a yardstick for our kids' growth and development. Children who sit rigidly on our laps, gripping our hands during the hayride one year are unafraid the next, nestling down in the brilliant yellow straw. I remember the time two-year-old Margaret wandered off while we waited in line at the cow-milking demonstration, and my heart nearly beat out of my chest while we looked for her. The experience reminded me once again that our sense of time is highly elastic and unreliable: the ninety seconds she was gone felt like an eternity. I still owe a thank-you to the woman who found her, but at the time I had no presence of mind to do anything but embrace my kid.

This year, as we pull into the parking lot and are waved into place by an orange-smocked attendant, we wonder whether our perennial activity will feel different with the "Sabbath" label on it.

I feel like my eyes and ears are open a little wider than they are normally; I'm led to pay more attention than I might have before. I notice the way James has no trace of baby left in him as he situates himself on a burlap sack at the top of the longest slide in the park. I notice the way Caroline reads the signs to her younger siblings with her clear and forthright voice. I notice Margaret's complete inability to see a hill or wall without climbing it.

I am not in charge today.

We go completely at the kids' pace. We do this partly because our kids are older and know the place well without our prompting and partly because this is a Sabbath activity. I am remembering my silliness at the children's festival last month, poring over the schedule, mapping our route. We discover that the kids' pace involves a good bit of doubling back, aimless wandering, and lingering at random attractions.

We also notice other parents hurrying their kids: "The hay ride line is short right now. Come on." In the past, we've been those parents, directing our kids, good-naturedly and gently (and sometimes not) to keep things moving. Every time I feel a prodding comment rise in my throat, I manage to swallow it down.

As we stroll through the park, we discover a whole section we've never seen: a place with "farm chores" such as pumping water and scooping up dried corn and placing it on a conveyor belt, only to have the corn spill back into the bin. Our kids spend more than thirty minutes collecting the corn and dumping it, using their sweatshirts as sacks for the dusty stuff. Even second-grader Caroline is down on her knees, gathering up big bunches and walking it to the belt. Back and forth.

With a start, I realize that my children are teaching me about the pleasure of simple repetitive tasks: the feel of the corn sifting through their fingers, the short journey back and forth, over and over. I wonder if I can remember this lesson the next time I make Caroline's PB&J.

The Sabbath label also gives us permission to keep it simple for lunch; we'd planned to go to a couple's house afterward. Instead of combing through the memory banks and cookbooks ahead of time for something to prepare, Robert stops by the grocery store for hot dogs and buns. We spend the rest of the day at their place carving pumpkins, lingering over beers, and disregarding naptime.

That night, I talk to Robert about something that's been bothering me: "These outings are fun, and they get me away from the house, which means I'm not tempted to work. But I struggle with doing Sabbath in a way that requires someone else to work."

"Hmm," he says, which is his "MaryAnn's about to overthink something" sound.

I go on. "We're relying on other people's work in order to have our Sabbath. We have this great experience that's obviously fun. But what about those workers? And their families? Shouldn't they get to enjoy some Sabbath too?"

"Well . . ." he pauses. "There's a recession going on. It's good that folks have jobs and are able to work. We don't want to minimize that. Our trip to the farm helps keep them employed."

"Eh, that's like people who say we should buy a lot of stuff at Christmas because stores rely on holiday sales to get them through the rest of the year. Just because this is the way it is doesn't mean it has to be this way."

I know that I am venturing out of my league. I'm no expert on the intricacies of the economy. But something isn't sitting quite right. I am rarely one to look back at the "good old days," but I understand why some folks pine for the time when stores, libraries, and movie theaters were closed on Sunday.

Part of what makes Sabbath so transformative for a community is that everyone is invited to participate. In many Jewish communities, people from all walks of life experience the rhythm of Sabbath meals, worship, and unhurried conversation. Whether the highest paid executive or the lowliest office worker, all have access to this weekly pause.

My question about the well-being of others on the Sabbath has its roots in Sabbath observance, too. One of the traditional rituals on Shabbat is placing coins in *tzedakah* boxes to give to people in need.[3] Sabbath is not an occasion for selfish, inwardly focused navel-gazing in which nobody else matters. Yes, we cease from the work of making the world a better place, but we continue to care about that world, because we believe that God cares about it and asks us to play a part in healing and transforming it.

At any rate, it feels a little Pharaoh-ish to have a carefree day with my family, made possible by the young people running the kettle corn machine. But I'm not sure what to do about that discomfort.

The Work of Sabbath: A Focus on Delight

Last month we started our experiment with a fairly straightforward definition of Sabbath: a time to stop. Sabbath invites us to take a day and not change anything—no bringing order to the chaos, no whittling away at the to-do list. But there are many ways to think about work and the contours of one's Sabbath.

According to the book of Isaiah in the Hebrew scriptures, we are to "delight" in the Sabbath:

> [I]f you call the Sabbath a delight
> and the holy day of the Lord honorable;
> if you honor it, not going your own ways,
> serving your own interests, or pursuing your own
>   affairs;
> then you shall take delight in the Lord . . . (Isa. 58:13)

I love the word "delight," with *light* embedded in it. Deeeee-light. Your mouth may decide to rebel and say, "Deeeee-licious," and that would be all right, too. Or you can morph it into an adjective and say that the Sabbath would be "delightful." Delight-full. Full, saturated, plump with goodness and joy.

Every now and then Robert and I reminisce about our top five days as a couple. It's fun to relive a fall day visiting wineries or a sunny afternoon snorkeling with giant sea turtles. After some twenty years together, there are way more delightful days than can fit in the top five, yet the list rarely changes. Something sets the top five days apart from other, merely good days. That "something" comes down to very basic elements: fresh air; nature; one another; and usually food and wine, consumed slowly enough to fully taste them. But above these basics hovers a sense of transcendence—the feeling of being loved by one another, sure, but also being part of a love that exists beyond us.

Our Sabbaths are attempts to take what's great about our top five days and create a space for a new one to occur without the exotic locale. Sabbath testifies that delight can happen without even leaving our street. Abraham Joshua Heschel writes that the Sabbath is "not a date but an atmosphere."[4] By focusing on delight, we create an atmosphere for something lovely to happen. Isaiah's words even suggest that when we take delight in the Sabbath, we experience the delight of God—they are one and the same.

After a month of Sabbath successes and failures, we are learning what brings us delight. We love listening to music. Cuddling with our kids. Singing together. Playing with blocks. Cooking and baking. Riding bicycles. Being together, out in the fresh air.

Delight also involves body-oriented joys that the church doesn't like to talk about, such as sex, which is viewed in Jewish circles as a mitzvah (good deed) on Shabbat.[5] Eating and napping are other bodily pleasures that bring delight as well, but they aren't usually named as spiritual practices in Christian literature, sadly.

Recently Robert has begun brewing beer. "It's like a chemistry set for grownups . . . with a tasty product to show for it," he says. As for me, I knit, badly, but am not too interested in improving. I let myself be bad at it, to enjoy it for its own sake. I like scarves—they require very little thought, just the same stitches, over and over. No counting, no keeping track of rows. I've made more complicated things, but scarves feel very Sabbath-friendly. By pursuing these delights—*oneg* in Hebrew, which means "pleasurable things"—we make the sabbath day holy.[6]

With a focus on delight, the invitation is to check oneself along the way: "Does what I'm doing right now bring delight?" Despite my love of the word, delight is often difficult for me; I find myself mired in "should." I'm not a gardener—I just don't enjoy it—yet somewhere I've picked up the notion that gardening is a thing that *real* adults do. But "should" has no place in Sabbath, especially a Sabbath focused on delight.

It feels like cheating to think about Sabbath as something that brings delight, that's free of obligation and "should." Religious disciplines are supposed to be rigorous, right?

Nah. Not this time. Isaiah says to delight, and delight we shall.

*   *   *

The next Sabbath, I am slated to lead a church women's retreat in the morning, something I agreed to do several months before our experiment started. No problem—the rest of the family will have a head start on Sabbath. Since it's a gorgeous day, sunny and mild, I expect I will have to meet them somewhere. Instead, as I leave the retreat I get a text that they're home. I walk in to chaos and hugs and a thin layer of flour on the kitchen counters.

Robert is a great father; he's patient and unflappable, especially in situations in which I am neither of these things. But today, he looks rumpled. "We got dressed and had breakfast, and I thought we'd go to the zoo since it's such a nice day. We were on our way out the door when Caroline decided she didn't want to go to the zoo after all. Pitched a complete fit. I didn't have the energy to fight that. Besides, part of the point is to have fun together, right? So I suggested hiking instead. Then it was Margaret who pitched the fit."

At this point both girls are looking sheepish. "I gave up. So yeah, it's a beautiful day and we're spending it inside. We decided to bake bread. We've had some fights over who would knead the dough, of course."

I wonder how much my being gone has thrown things off. Maybe even recreation becomes work with a one-to-three parent-to-child ratio.

Later Robert and I debrief the day. We don't normally change our plans because a kid stomps her feet and sulks. Maybe Robert could have pressed on, unwilling to let Caroline hijack the day, hopeful that she would snap out of it. Besides, with three kids, someone's always disappointed. If we wait for unanimity, we'll never do anything.

But maybe Sabbath plays by different rules. If the focus is on delight, isn't the point to enjoy one another? And isn't it much more enjoyable to minimize the drama however we can?

Or is that not even possible with young children?

*   *   *

As we settle into our yearlong experiment, I take comfort in how Jesus approaches the Sabbath in scripture. He doesn't always observe the sabbath day the way people want him to; he's constantly getting in trouble for healing on the Sabbath, for example. He declares, "The Sabbath was made for humankind, and not humankind for the Sabbath," which suggests to me that we are free to make Sabbath our own (Mk. 2:27).

Jesus seems to do that, too. He takes Sabbath seriously while still finding his own way. He doesn't postpone Sabbath until everyone has been tended to. He doesn't cross everything off the messianic to-do list, nod, and say, "Now. Sabbath can begin." He just *goes*–to the mountain, to a deserted place. And people don't always understand it or make it easy on him. At one point, he comes back from one of these retreats to find the disciples saying, "Everyone is searching for you!" (Mk. 1:37).

Thanks to my children, I hear the disciples' statement in an accusatory way. It's the tone my kids take when they can't find me for five minutes: "Where were you? We were looking all over for you!"

I was in the basement folding clothes.

I was in the bathroom, for heaven's sake.

Jesus dismisses crowds filled with people still aching to be healed in order to get away for restoration. He sneaks out first thing in the morning, before folks have a chance to corner him with more and more need. He goes by himself. He prays.

Jesus manages to carve out the time for Sabbath, despite the dire needs that confront him at every turn. I have a hard enough time setting aside trivial things: the mail on the kitchen table, begging to be sorted, or the pile of Brownie patches that need to be sewn onto Caroline's sash.

Not exactly life-or-death stuff.

*   *   *

Next Sabbath, there's a rally downtown on the National Mall hosted by Jon Stewart and Stephen Colbert, two of our favorite comedians. We really want to go, but we are determined to do it Sabbathly: we decide to stay as long as the kids can stand it, then leave. Sometimes it takes us so much work to get somewhere that we feel like we need to stay a good long while to make it worth the trouble. But this time Robert says, "If we only stay for an hour, that's still more than we would've had if we hadn't gone at all." And sure enough, the crowds and the noise are such that the kids make it about ninety minutes before they're ready to go. As we saunter back to the Metro, we get a kick out of the swarms of people, all good natured and holding hilarious signs. We bask in the sunshine and hear occasional snippets of music as we wind through the crowd.

We are feeling pretty proud of ourselves for not overdoing it. But it's a beautiful day and we aren't ready to go home; it is still midafternoon. So we go to a park near our house that has an ice cream parlor, a carousel, and a train. It is Halloween weekend, so we ride the Ghost Train, featuring characters in costume who act out silly scenes. The girls know the ropes, but James is enchanted, especially by the fistful of candy corn he receives at the end of the ride.

Sabbath ends, and Sunday is a full day—Halloween. When we get home from church we realize we absolutely have to get started on raking leaves, and there are costumes to finish. The girls are Lucy and Susan Pevensie from the *Chronicles of Narnia* books, and while we'd ordered dresses online, Susan needs a bow and arrows, and Lucy needs her healing potion. We find an old green glass medicine bottle that will do the trick. I enjoy the challenge of using what we have around the house and the simple pleasure of making something with the girls, but the afternoon evaporates quickly. Thank goodness James's Thomas the Tank Engine costume requires no embellishments. We barely finish the jack-o'-lantern before trick-or-treaters begin to arrive, princesses and Darth Vaders picking their way up our sidewalk.

It's a full weekend, crammed to the brim with fun and memories. That night, Robert and I collapse into bed. Despite our efforts to pace ourselves, it was all too much. Even the Sabbath, as fun as it was, felt consumed, not experienced. We are like a sponge that has been wrung out.

Was it too much of a good thing? Or has the Sabbath changed us such that we can't go at the pace we used to? Has something begun to happen after only two months?

Sabbath Hack: Map the Boundaries

For Jews, the boundaries of Sabbath come ready-made. They may be adapted for specific situations, but the parameters are there. Sabbath begins on Friday near sundown with a special meal, prayers, and the lighting of candles. Children receive a special blessing.

The next day is spent with family and friends. There may be study of the Torah and lively discussion. Folks go to synagogue that day—those who live close by can walk—and many linger after services. People open their homes to guests.

From the beginning of our family's experiment, we have felt the need and responsibility to find our own rhythm rather than copying the Jewish way. We must establish our own boundaries.

The word "boundary" can feel oppressive to people—limits often seem punitive, and establishing rigid boundaries can set us up for failure when we don't "get it right."

For folks who bristle at the idea of boundaries, my friend Julie Johnson has suggested thinking of a boundary not as a brick wall but as a coastline where water and dry land come together.

I like this image. There is constancy in the coastline, but it also changes. The beach constantly shifts under the power of the wind, waves, and tides. Sand washes out to sea and is redeposited by the surf. Dunes are formed, unformed, and reformed. The beach is the same yet is never quite the same. The image honors the unpredictability of life, especially life with children.

This is helpful as I think about our Sabbath practice. We have boundaries, but they have flexibility built into them:

We plan on Thursday what our weekend will look like, including Sabbath . . . but there's always wiggle room in our plans.

Our Sabbath begins on Saturday morning . . . unless we are ready even earlier, in which case it begins in the dark quiet of Friday night.

Sabbath ends for us when the children are in bed Saturday evening . . . generally, but sometimes not. (Having Saturday night as an optional time to work gives me a chance to finish writing my sermon, if I wasn't able to do it earlier.)

We do not work on Sabbath . . . but there are times when it makes sense to do so.

Sometimes we stay home. Sometimes we go somewhere together as a family. Our activities vary from week to week, but hopefully, the common elements are togetherness, intention, and mindfulness.

Each individual and family must map their own boundary waters when it comes to Sabbath and time. Here are some questions to consider in charting the coastline:

- How long will the Sabbath be?
- When will it begin?

- Will the Sabbath be the same day each week?
- If the time frame needs to shift, when and how will that be decided?
- When will the work that normally takes place on the sabbath day occur?
- Will the Sabbath time involve a communal activity? Or will each person do his/her own thing? Or a combination?
- How will the Sabbath time begin? With the lighting of a candle? A ringing bell? A time of silence? A song?
- Will there be devotions, prayers, or other traditional religious activities? (Our family keeps things light with our Sabbath. We believe that activities deemed "secular" have the sacred nestled within them, if we have eyes to see. A life well lived can be a prayer of praise.)
- How will the Sabbath end?

For us, one of the most important questions is what to do when we miss a Sabbath—we have already done so and will again. Our answer? We begin anew the next week.

*   *   *

Occasionally I meet people who are intrigued by Sabbath but they feel that it's too late. The ship has sailed in their family's life; perhaps their children are too old for such a radical shift. "My teenagers would never agree to it" is a common response. I can't claim to know what it's like to parent teenagers. I suspect forcing them to observe Sabbath would backfire spectacularly.

But this objection reminds me of a parenting workshop I attended many years ago. The leader asked us to write down our goals and hopes for our children as they grow up. What would we like to see for them at age twenty-one?

It was a heartwarming experience to imagine our children on the verge of being launched, all full of glowing potential without the messy inconvenience of reality mucking up the fantasy. My list was filled with lofty goals—that they would understand their strengths and limitations, that they would have a spirit of service toward others, and so forth. (Later, I asked Robert what he would wish for our children—what success would look like at age twenty-one. Without hesitation he said, "Their own apartment.")

After writing our lists, the workshop participants read them to one another and basked in the radiance of all these self-actualized

Eagle Scouts and lacrosse captains, confident yet humble. They were like young adult ghosts, beaming all around us. Then the leader said something that made them all disappear: *Poof!*

"This list is for you," she said. "You want your children to have a spirit of service? A sense of the Holy? A curiosity and openness to the world? Cultivate those things for yourself. Let them see you do it. Become the parent and person you want to be. It's one of the most important things you can do for your child."

I sometimes tell this story to parents of teens. If you want your teenager to have an understanding of Sabbath, I say, if you want her to understand time as more than a container for text messages and drama tournaments and papers, then start with yourself. Take Sabbath yourself—an hour, an afternoon, a day. Maybe they will follow your example. Probably they won't, but perhaps a seed is planted. Or maybe time spent in rest will allow you to be a more present, relaxed parent. We start with ourselves—we're the only people we can really control anyway. To paraphrase the poet Mary Oliver: through Sabbath, we save the only lives we can save.[7]

4

November

Life moves pretty fast. If you don't stop and look around once in a while, you could miss it.

—Ferris Bueller[1]

A pastor friend likes to dismiss his congregation at the end of the worship service by saying, "Now go out into the world to love God and love your neighbor. It's all that easy . . . and it's all that hard."

The same can be said of Sabbath.

Two months in, we've already botched the call to weekly rest. We've also had flashes of luminosity, in which we looked around and sighed with satisfaction. But those moments were fleeting.

Despite these stops and starts, I have to think that Sabbath is worth the struggle. The victory is in showing up and making oneself available. Just as Robert and I make ourselves available to one another, having at least a short conversation each night before sleep claims us. Just as I seek to be present with my kids, not because every moment will feel holy and blessed but because holy and blessed moments don't happen unless I *am* present.

"There are some things that spontaneity simply cannot offer," Blu Greenberg writes about the ritualistic aspect of Shabbat. "[Sabbath provides] a steadiness and stability which . . . at best, creates the possibility of investing time with special meaning, experience with special value, and life with a moment of transcendence."[2] And so we will keep showing up to each other—and to Sabbath.

November, month three, will bring its own peculiar challenges. It can be a busy time in the church as we plan for the Advent and Christmas seasons. The leaves are falling fast and furious and take hours each weekend to manage: blowing, raking, and bagging. It's the little things too: the weather shifts, and Caroline's bare legs get gooseflesh at the bus stop in the morning. Time to dig out the winter clothes and take inventory of the bag of mittens to see which ones had mates that skipped town.

November is my favorite month, a rustle of red, gold, and brown between the brilliance of October and the twinkling lights of December. If I blink, it will be New Year's Day. Sabbath feels like a way to stall, to slow down time a little so that I don't miss a beloved time of the year.

*   *   *

This month, for the first time since our experiment began, we take a Sunday Sabbath instead of a Saturday one. (Caroline protests: "We can't take a Sabbath on Sunday! That's all wrong!" Err, clearly some more education is needed on this whole Sabbath thing. I try to explain that Sunday is actually traditional—we're in the minority among Christians.)

Sunday Sabbath makes Saturday a leaf day. The trees in our yard refuse to respect the fact that we have one fewer day a weekend to deal with their output. I am stunned at their betrayal, but we cannot ignore the yellow-and-orange carpet around our house any longer.

The kids are ecstatic. "LEAF PILE!" Margaret shrieks in anticipation. James echoes his big sister, despite the fact that at two, he has no memory of what a leaf pile is.

We have a lazy morning and get a late start on the outdoor chores. Maybe the routine of Saturday Sabbath is already seeping into us? Whatever the reason, there's only a short time to get it all done. I come outside after cleaning and decluttering the first floor, another chore we've been putting off. The kids have convinced Robert to make a gigantic pile and rerake after each exuberant leap. They emerge, oak and maple leaves clinging to hair and jackets. I try not to think about sharp sticks lurking in all that crinkly joyfulness.

We're losing our daylight fast, and there's still the backyard to finish. Robert heads back there with the leaf blower, the extension cord snaking around the side of the house.

Later he comes in, flushed and smelling of autumn. It is twilight. "Check it out," he says, grinning and nodding toward the kitchen window.

I look at the backyard. There is a line across the length of the backyard. He's blown half the leaves and left the other half of the yard intact.

"I didn't finish," he shrugs happily. "Oh well."

I marvel at his ability to leave something so visibly undone. "Wow, you are so much less compulsive than me. I love it."

"It would probably take me twenty minutes to finish it up tomorrow. I know it's Sabbath though."

"Well, whatever you want to do."

On Sabbath he bakes a pie instead.

*   *   *

I am in a Bible study with a group of pastors, and we're studying the verse "Teach us to count our days" from Psalm 90. We wonder what it might have meant back then. I know what it means to me now: to make our days count. To view time not as something cheap and disposable but as priceless.

As we talk, someone pulls up a quote on her smartphone that's floated around the Internet, attributed to Hunter S. Thompson: "Life should not be a journey to the grave with the intention of arriving safely in a pretty and well-preserved body, but rather to skid in broadside in a cloud, thoroughly used up, totally worn out, and loudly proclaiming 'Wow! What a Ride!'"

A couple of people laugh. One nods in agreement. And someone says, "It's a good one. I'm all for making the most of life. All we have is now, right? But I don't think this gets the tone right."

"Yes!" I say, with Sabbath on the brain. "If we live a long life, chances are it won't end that way. We're not going to slide into death in a cloud of smoke, or whatever it says. It will be quiet and surrounded with friends and family. If we're lucky."

Someone adds, "So the trick is to live life to the fullest, but in a deliberate way . . . not desperately, like we have to beat the clock."

Another chimes in, "Yeah, let's not forget that Hunter Thompson killed himself, poor guy. Not exactly 'counting one's days.'"

We keep going, drilling down, digging deeper into the psalm. *Teach us to count our days.*

Finally someone pipes up: "Maybe life isn't a series of calendar pages to be ripped off one by one. Maybe life is a journal page to be filled. Maybe that's what the psalmist is saying."

In two sentences, my friend has described the heart of our family's Sabbath project: to make time our friend, not our enemy.

I think about my great grandmother, who had dozens of family members together celebrating her ninetieth birthday when I was a kid. Someone said, "Grandma, how about going for a hundred?" She looked up and said quietly, "I haven't decided whether I'm going to do one hundred yet." I was touched that she knew that her time was finite and she was at peace with it. In counting her days, she knew she'd had a gracious plenty of them and didn't need to go for the next milestone.

It's the "totally worn out" part of the quote that gets under my skin. My life is "worn out," and it happens through so many small decisions. Should we attend the optional Brownie activity? How about checking e-mail one last time before bed? Or saying yes to one more church committee assignment?

Something's pulling me away from Hunter Thompson and toward the psalm. Count our days. Make them count. Be awake.

I think about this push and pull as I consider Halloween weekend and how full it was. Before the Sabbath experiment, it would have been a normal weekend. Now a weekend like that leaves me feeling depleted, not energized. We're getting into the busiest time of year, and we have to be more intentional. Halloween was a poke on the shoulder—*this will not do.*

Teach me to count my days.

*   *   *

Our weekly Sabbath practice gets sidetracked because of a family wedding in New York City. We take the train from DC to Penn Station, which delights James, lover of all things locomotive. Then we meet up with Robert's family for the wedding festivities—a tea at a local restaurant, dinner afterward, and the wedding the next day, with reception that goes late into the night.

It is tantalizing to be in New York for the first time as a family. Growing up in Houston, New York was the stuff of romantic comedies: a faraway, mythical place, immense and pulsing with activity. There's so much to do and see. And there are just enough open spaces during the weekend that we are tempted to fill the time with tourist activities. After all, getting the five of us up there is no small matter. Shouldn't we make the most of it?

I remember the psalm: *teach us to count our days.* We decide to keep it simple: we do a little exploring around our hotel, but we decide to focus on family and the wedding. A friend of mine tells me her mother's declarations while on vacation: "Let's leave something for next time." It occurs to me how counterintuitive that is. Sometimes there isn't a next time. Yet the best approach to travel is to savor and enjoy a place, not gorge on it. Much like life.

We do schedule one nonwedding activity: some time at a local park with a friend who lives in New York plus his two boys. He's a writer, musician, and sole proprietor of a fledgling small business. His wife is a singer with a day job that pays the bills. The children—both his and ours—climb the jungle gym, come back to home base for snacks, and are back again, digging in the sand. Inevitably the conversation comes around to the sabbath experiment.

I am starting to open up more with folks about our sabbath project. I've blogged about it, but it's harder to talk about face to face. It has felt too new, too fragile. We haven't felt experienced enough to field a bunch of questions and skepticism. Now that we have a few months under our belt, we can talk about it more.

But I am ambivalent as a sabbath evangelist. I realize how fortunate I am to be able to take an entire day. My life is set up for it. I work part time, a decision we made when James was born, which means that weekend time does not have to be quite so jammed full of errands. The church I serve is small, with fewer weekend activities and meetings than larger congregations. It is rare that I get a call from a parishioner on the Sabbath, though the potential is always there.

But what about others whose lives *aren't* set up for it?

My friend and I get to talking about the Jewish Shabbat. I am marveling at the prohibitions—the thirty-nine activities that are forbidden on the Sabbath—and I admit my envy at having things all spelled out, though I'd find a stringent Sabbath hard to pull off.

My friend, who is Jewish, deadpans, "The thing you need to understand is that Jews find stress relaxing." I laugh.

"But seriously," he goes on, "It wouldn't work for our family. In this economy, we're making ends meet. Sabbath is a privilege when you're self-employed. If I take time off, that's money I don't make. And my wife is at the beck and call of the corporate overlords. If they need her to work on the weekend, she works on the weekend. They don't care if we have something planned."

Part of his wife's job is to design PowerPoint slides. We joke about that being the definition of a soul-sucking job, but the conversation has left me uneasy. Robert and I have mucked up Sabbath a few times, but I've also seen glimpses of how beautiful it can be. It's a simple pleasure that's totally free . . . except that it isn't, not for people whose livelihoods depend on constant availability.

On the train ride home from New York, with an exhausted James asleep on my lap, I think about the conversation with my friend and the objections I sometimes hear to the idea of Sabbath. Some people react with defensiveness, as if our family's practice is somehow a judgment on their own lives. Other folks like to ferret out any bits of work we do in order to bring the experience down to size. Our kids watch television sometimes. We cook. We drive. *Cheaters!*

Some people make a game out of pointing out another person's hypocrisy, like folks who love to crow over leather shoes on the feet of a vegetarian. I don't find that very sporting, since our world is complicated, and I've never met a completely consistent person. I want to say, "Yes, I'm a hypocrite. Big surprise. So is everyone you meet." Our actions and beliefs so rarely harmonize perfectly. Yet it is worthwhile to *try* to bring them into congruence.

By far the most popular reaction to Sabbath is similar to my friend's: "Sounds nice . . . but we don't have time."

I don't have time. It's a curious phrase. Do any of us *have* time? Is time something we possess? Is it a commodity, a thing to own? It may be more accurate to say that time has us. Time holds us in its dispassionate grip. Time has its way with us. We work. We age. Our children grow up and leave us, which I keep hearing happens much sooner than we think. Sabbath is the only tool in my arsenal for fighting back.

Margaret is flitting across the aisle of the train, bouncing between me and Robert. I pull a coloring book out of my bag and she settles in next to me, tucking her feet underneath her and pushing her brown hair behind her ears. She traces the words on the title page, making shaky outlines of the letters.

Sometimes when people tell me they don't have time, I think about the story of Jesus and the man who could not walk. Jesus asks him, "Do you want to be made well?" In response, the man comes up with reasons why he's not able to be healed, even though he is sitting on the bank of a pool that is said to contain healing waters (Jn. 5:1–9).

I feel the tension in my own life. I want to live abundantly and relish this time of our lives. But I can think of all sorts of reasons—excuses—why it's simply not possible. Thankfully, Jesus cuts through the man's excuses and heals him anyway. And in an ironic twist, he heals him on the Sabbath. He gets in trouble for this with the authorities, who begin "persecuting" him for his bad timing (Jn. 5:16).

I've wondered at the fact that Jesus does so much healing on the Sabbath. It feels like a clue, whispered to me from the pages of scripture: new life and transformation can come to us on and through that day. Healing and Sabbath go hand in hand.

Do we want life to be different than it is? Do we want our relationship with time to be different?

If the answer is no, that's OK. No guilt. Some people are wired a different way.

Others, however, want to change . . . but still insist they don't have time.

I have a friend who is a single parent. Her work schedule does not allow for many errands during the week. Sunday she works as a substitute preacher at various churches in the area. These gigs can sometimes stretch into the afternoon. This leaves Saturday as the only day to visit the Laundromat and grocery store.

Then there's my friend in New York. Being self-employed means he's flexible, which means he can take time off as needed. But that time off comes at a cost that is much more direct than an office worker who has paid time off.

Some circumstances do not lend themselves to a weekly, day-long Sabbath. I wonder for those folks, if it's possible to take one of those adjectives away. Take away "weekly" and do it every three weeks. Or take away "daylong" and make it only a few hours of time set aside, claimed as Sabbath.

I have a friend who's a doctor in a hospital emergency room. She's one of the busiest people I know. She and her husband work conflicting schedules, which makes a family Sabbath impossible. Instead she takes "Sabbath time," which she puts in quotes because it's not a full day and not always on the same day of the week. "My son and I read, sing, put together puzzles, make cookies, go to the museum, tromp through the woods. Nothing that needs to be scheduled unless it is wonderful and joyous—like a puppet parade this weekend." I love it.

I look out the train window at the backsides of houses as they whizz by.

Other people I know say they don't have time, but they probably do—they just don't see a way out of the way things are.

It's true that changing one's life takes a lot of mental energy. We also have to reach the point where the status quo costs us more than the effort required to make a change.

There's an insidious keeping-up-with-the-Joneses thing that is very hard to fight when it comes to raising children. It's not solely giving one's kids the latest toys or the nicest clothes. A lot of one-upmanship isn't about stuff; it's about experiences and opportunities. You don't want your kid in three sports, but that's what others around you are doing. Dance lessons . . . scouting . . . language classes . . . It's possible to step out of the activities, or to dramatically reduce them, but it's a lonely place to be. Some would consider it parental malpractice not to give your kid as many opportunities as you could handle.

Sabbath is pretty straightforward for us now, I think. But what about when they're all in school, each with their own activities? Maybe I'll be one of those people too, saying "I don't have time."

The train pulls into a station, and James stirs. I shift in my seat, uncomfortable under his weight, but also unsettled by my lack of answers to these questions.

The Work of Sabbath: Bringing Life Back into Balance

As our experiment evolves, so has our understanding of what Sabbath is about. In September we thought about Sabbath as a time to stop trying to change things, to let things be. In October it was a focus on delight, to find things we enjoy.

This month I'm feeling weighed down by the questions. What activities are in or out? What constitutes work? Are my kids spending too much time in front of the television? Are all these family field trips missing the point? I'm so busy evaluating that I'm forgetting to live. Perhaps I need Sabbath as a time to bring life back into some balance. It's time to let go of all the questions and get swept along in Sabbath-keeping, whatever that might look like.

"I'm tired of talking about and thinking about Sabbath," I tell Robert the week after New York. "I think it's possible to be *too* intentional!"

"Well. Sounds like it's time to be unintentional."

So I spend the next Sabbath in my pajamas, puttering. I page through a stack of magazines with my feet propped up in the chair that gets all the bright autumn light. The girls play Go Fish–Margaret's hands are too small for the cards, so she lays them out behind the toy piano so Caroline can't see them–while James sets up his cars in elaborate traffic jams around his Fisher-Price airport. Meanwhile, Robert starts a new batch of beer. I look up from my reading every now and then and smile in spite of myself. Who knew heaven was a place that smelled like liquid bread, that featured *Real Simple* and *O Magazine* as reading material? Who knew we'd wear purple fleece robes up there instead of the gauzy white ones like those in so many *New Yorker* cartoons?

The phone rings. Caroline is invited to go to an indoor pool with a friend. I stop to consider. *Wait, isn't Sabbath family time? Ugh, stop thinking so much!* We say yes, and she bounds upstairs to find her swimsuit. After she leaves, I let Margaret and James drag me downstairs, where we take turns playing *Wii Sport Resort.* At two, James loves the airplane game but is too young to manage the controls. When the plane crashes, the person bounces out of the cockpit with a parachute and a BOING sound. James dissolves into giggles again and again. So why help him? His laughter is irresistible.

When it seems like they've had enough, I give them the five-minute warning, then we turn it off. Amazingly, there are no tears or protests. Are they more relaxed because I am?

I am filled with gratitude. That our family has decided to do this every week–and that the God we affirm actually *commands* us to do so–gives me a wonderful feeling. The day is thick with peace.

When our lives feel out of balance, when we've gotten off track from our true north, Sabbath can be a day to tip things back in the other direction, to bring things into balance.

The possibilities are endless:

Too much tweeting and Facebooking? Addicted to the twenty-four-hour news cycle? Tip the balance by finding a good long book to read on Sabbath. (Some folks who are particularly Internet-addled may need to choose a book they know really well. It might be too hard to dive into something brand new.)

Peopled out? Find balance by setting aside some time during the Sabbath to be undisturbed. (A challenge with children, but there are ways. I'm not above bribery on the Sabbath: "Give Mommy and Daddy one hour of uninterrupted time and we'll have brownie sundaes for dinner.")

Tired of breathing stale office air? Get outside.

Sedentary at a desk? Make Sabbath a time to move, whether it's dancing in the living room or walking the neighborhood.

And too many Sabbath field trips? Spend some time at home, which is what we end up doing a lot in November. It is freeing.

*   *   *

I've been hearing about no-knead bread on blogs and cooking shows. I've always liked the *idea* of bread-making but had long ago written it off as not my thing. I'd tried once and failed once, as a newlywed, for a bridal shower Robert and I were hosting. I never could get the yeast to proof—the water was too warm, or too cold, or too *something*. Too wrong. Too amateurish. So I moved on to the other preparations for the shower and swore off the bread-making enterprise without looking back. "Eh, I don't bake bread," I would tell people with not a trace of sadness. It felt liberating: *Here's something I can cross off my list, something I don't need to master.* I mentally delegated bread to the grocery store or the bakery a few miles from our house.

But now Sabbath gives me permission to try again, and I'm almost hoping the recipe flops. A little failure is good for the perfectionist soul, especially on Sabbath. It'll be another good way to bring life into balance: to try something new, to be a novice, and to do it in front of my children.

I assemble a batch using one of the no-knead recipes and put it away for eighteen hours per the instructions. Sure enough, the dough never rises.

"Hmm . . . I wonder if it's a little too chilly in here for it to rise properly," says Robert, the chef in the family. He peers down at the tiny ball, lazing in the bowl. "Let's see . . . oh, I bet I can figure something out!" He disappears into the basement for a couple of hours.

When I come down later, I laugh at his contraption—a large Rubbermaid tub with wires poking out of it and something taped to the inside of the lid. "All right, MacGyver, what's this?"

"It's a bread-rising cabinet!" he announces. "I had a leftover timer and thermostat, and you remember that old heating pad? So I rigged up the heating pad to the thermostat so it will keep the temperature constant, and taped the heating pad to the lid. Voila–seventy-five degrees, no matter how cool it gets in the house."

My husband spends his week in meetings, writing product requirements, interacting with customers, and cajoling software developers to make their deadlines. It's hard, cerebral, extroverted work. Maybe his hands-on tinkering brings some balance to his life.

So we're off. And the contraption works! The next week I put the dough together on the Sabbath, knowing it won't be ready to bake until the next day. This pleases me; it's as if the Sabbath spills over to the next day–despite whatever busyness we're managing, there will be a mound of leftover Sabbath, cooling on the counter.

The bread is spongy, simple, and delicious. It tastes wholesome, uncomplicated.

The following week, I time the bread differently. Instead of putting together the dough on the Sabbath, I prepare it ahead of time for baking on the Sabbath. That makes the Sabbath a day of surprise–what will I find when I open Robert's Handy-Dandy Bread Cabinet? I pull out the little loaf-to-be, knead it ten to fifteen times, put it in a cast-iron skillet for a second rise, then bake it in a Dutch oven. Success!

The recipe says to mix the ingredients into a "shaggy loaf." That fits me. I feel shaggy a lot of the time. The dough is not a beautiful thing. It's got bumps and crevices. There's no way to predict what will happen during its eighteen hours of rest. It might plump up, full of bubbles, effervescent, transformed. Or it might stay the same, squat and unchanged. I can't predict why it works sometimes and not others. Just like some Sabbaths are better than others.

I see why Jewish observances of Shabbat include bread–big yeasty braids of challah. And the ritual of hand-washing prior to breaking bread and eating makes sense to me. The practice originated with notions of purity that aren't as strictly observed anymore. But the idea of preparing oneself to eat bread appeals to me as I behold my miraculous little loaf. *I made that,* I think. But I'm not the sole creator.

It seems that there are three elements to baking bread: the raw ingredients, the effort of the bread baker, and the mysterious third factor, time. We bring what we can to the recipe, but time will have its way with it. We can't rush things; nor can we predict what the hours will do. The bread, and we, must wait.

Sit.

Rest.

This is my life. I have my raw ingredients: Spouse. Children. Work. Family and friends. What I do with those ingredients is up to me. I can pour and mix, then overknead the dough until my shoulders ache. All that effort will make me feel productive, but it will ruin it; life will feel hard and heavy and the result will not nourish. Instead, I need to let time, in all its mysteries, have its way with me. Sometimes the outcome will be light and airy, studded with bubbles. Sometimes it will be thick and dense, substantial but tough.

Either way, I have to let it be.

Sabbath Hack: TV Tokens

It's Thanksgiving weekend, as well as James's third birthday. The weekend is a tumble of feasts and leftovers, Christmas decorations, a Thomas ice cream cake, and a few errands and chores. Once again, we find ourselves remapping the boundary waters in a way that makes sense for us. We decide to sprinkle Sabbath moments throughout the four days rather than partitioning a single day.

Long weekends are the times our kids get especially crazy over the television, asking to watch it constantly, whining when it's time to turn it off. At the same time, they see Robert and me checking Facebook on our phones and answering e-mail. Clearly we need to think about the role of technology on the Sabbath.

I'm not ready to quit cold turkey and not even sure we should, so I come up with a solution. After conferencing with Robert, I call the troops together.

"OK, guys. This weekend we're going to try something new with the TV. Each of you will receive one coin each day, which you can spend on thirty minutes of television or thirty minutes of a video game. When the token is spent, screen time is over."

"Can we watch each other's shows?" asks Caroline, ever the litigator.

"Yes, but each kid gets to make his or her own decision. No big kids putting pressure on the little ones."

I give Caroline a dime, Margaret a nickel, and James a penny. Predictably, they want to spend their coins immediately.

But to my amazement, the strategy works. And it works again the next day, and the next. They hand over the coins that I have pressed into their palms. Later, they fill those empty palms with other things: a paintbrush, a toy boat, a book. And there is no nagging for the rest of the day.

I crow about my inspired solution to a friend of mine, a Seventh-Day Adventist who grew up with a strict Sabbath. She laughs and pretends to give me a hard time: "Wait, not only are your kids watching TV, but there's money involved? So you're doing commerce *and* television? On the Sabbath?!"

I don't care what she says. It's a Sabbath miracle.

* * *

After three months of Sabbath, it's hard to generalize about the experience. There are times I feel a sweet calmness descending from out of nowhere—not only on Sabbath but on other days, too. Other times I feel crabby with a side of unease over the little maintenance tasks we are falling behind on. Robert's hair is starting to look shaggy—it's hard to find time for a haircut during the week and the barber is open on Saturday but not Sunday. Our van's inspection sticker expires, which I discover when a police officer pulls me over—while in the McDonald's drive-thru.

The Talmud, which is the collection of Jewish wisdom assembled and distilled by rabbis over a period of centuries, says that to study is the highest commandment. It's what Jews are called to do on Shabbat. Some books even provide study guides and suggested quotations to get folks started.

I guess I am studying Sabbath each week. I study it the way a biologist might study ants or zebra fish: with curiosity and no small bit of reverence.

I study the way the sunlight crawls across the kitchen as our family lingers over breakfast with nowhere to be.

I study the hole that is forming in my leather slippers from wearing them each week.

I study the hard brown crust of the bread and the puff of steam that escapes when we cut into it because we can't wait for it to cool.

I study the hunched forms of Robert and Margaret as they color together. When they show off their drawing later, I see the invisible line down the middle where his precise lines and shapes meet the lovely scrawls of a four-year-old.

I study Caroline's crossed legs in footy pajamas as she reads the latest *A to Z Mystery* in the corner of the room.

I study the ways I feel irritated for no good reason. I study the ways I resist breathing deeply.

I study the role of music on the Sabbath. I study my delight at coming up with the right music that encapsulates the energy and luxuriousness of the day.

I study my twitchiness when I'm feeling bored and ready to check e-mail or Facebook.

I study what happens in me when Margaret asks me to read her a story or James asks me to build a train track for him. I study the way that my mouth begins to form, "Not right now," when there is no reason to put them off. The reflex to be doing something else is so strong.

I study my satisfaction at saying yes to them.

5

December

Fling wide the portals of your heart
Make it a temple, set apart
From early use for heaven's employ
Adorned with prayer, and love, and joy.

—GEORG WEISSEL[1]

Growing up, our family's Christmas Open House was always my favorite holiday tradition. I liked it better than the visit to the mall Santa; better than driving around to look at Christmas lights, deliciously past bedtime; better even than decorating the tree.

Open House meant a house full of people for the better part of a Sunday. My father, a salesman by profession, would mingle in the crowd. My baby brothers' jobs were simply to be their cute selves. My little sister was in charge of the guest book, and she would collect a hundred or more names from the neighborhood, church, Dad's work, Girl Scouts, school, and sports teams.

My job was music. I would stack up several records at a time on the player and plan an eclectic assortment of tunes: John Denver's *Rocky Mountain Christmas*, followed by Handel's *Messiah*, followed by a cheap Burl Ives record my mother got free with a tank of gas at the Shell station. I would adjust the volume as necessary when conversation got loud or quiet. (I'm still the one who selects the playlist on Sabbath and other times for our family. Everyone's life needs a good soundtrack.)

My mother had the largest job by far: food. We had to put an extra leaf in the table, beyond even what we needed as a family of six, to hold everything she prepared. Mom worked for days getting ready, poring over cookbooks for new recipes to try. December afternoons would find her slicing and baking homemade cheese crackers, stirring bubbling pots of brown sugar and buttermilk for pralines, and forming tiny meatballs that would simmer in the slow cooker before being speared with colored toothpicks. On nights I couldn't sleep, I'd come downstairs and find the kitchen light blazing and my mother stirring, slicing, and measuring.

This was what my mother, who grew up in the 1950s, had been trained to do—not the Open House specifically, but the domestic tasks of running a family and a household. She made lunches, sewed clothes, volunteered at the school, and cooked.

When my parents divorced in the mid-1980s, my mother stopped cooking. It's an exaggeration to say that she never again darkened a kitchen, but the difference was dramatic. There was a clear Before and After. Once the 1950s dream ended, she turned off the oven and hung up the apron. She was done.

I think about this Before and After every December. Did she resent the Christmas Open House all those years? Or did she enter a new phase of life that involved full-time work and supporting four children, a phase in which she could credibly give up Swedish meatballs and wassail? Did she have no tools for asking for help, no models of hospitality other than frantic and solitary activity? (Heaven forbid we should have a potluck!)

Above all, I wonder, did she ever truly rest from her work?

My mother is thankfully very much alive, but her Ghost of Christmas Past haunts me every December. I'm one of those hopeless holiday types who can't get enough of Christmas music and the general hustle and bustle. I love the month-long bake-a-thon and parade of holiday gatherings.

But December is my nemesis, too. The month trumpets its expectations in a raucous parade of Christmas jingles, catalogs, and cards: to cram the time with memories, to be creative and resourceful. December should be home-cooked when possible and prepackaged only when necessary. If you do it "right," December is Ball jars, candy thermometers, and homemade gift cards.

December is also a growing mountain of cardboard from the Amazon.com boxes that invade our home. December is realizing at the last minute that I've forgotten a gift for the piano teacher or the Brownie leader. December is stress and the ever-increasing sense that there is something unholy about the frenetic run-up to Christmas. December is feeling the heaviness of folks around me who hate the holidays, who are estranged from family members, or who are missing a loved one long gone.

December is also a hard time for pastors. It's a busy time, triggering whiplash in those of us who cling to the hushed expectancy of the Advent season while everyone else is binging on Christmas cheer all month. "Let every heart prepare him room," we sing in the beloved Christmas carol . . . but how much space is there, really, when our rooms are already crammed floor to ceiling with other stuff?

I applaud my mother for finding her way into her authentic self, even as it colors my memories of the Christmas Open House. I am determined to avoid, if possible, such a clear Before and After. I want to experience this December, and all the Decembers to come, as occasions for stress-free joy. I want to celebrate the holidays in ways that are sustainable, in every sense of the word.

This year, Sabbath will be a vital ingredient in the mix. I suspect that our days will still be holly-jolly, but at a speed that's somewhere south of "breakneck." Maybe every day can be that way. Here's hoping.

* * *

Early in the month, a friend sends me an article on happiness. Just in time for the Christmas shopping season, a new study shows that we receive more satisfaction when we spend money on experiences (vacations, outings, recreation) than on things. Our cultural intuition suggests that physical stuff would make us happier longer, while experiences fade over time. But according to the study, the opposite is true: our enjoyment of objects decreases, while our memories of an experience deepen. What's more, we typically receive more pleasure from spending a *little bit* of money on experiences than spending *extravagant* money on objects. We get more bang for our buck with doing, not possessing.[2]

The study has obvious implications for Sabbath and our sense of time. We can spend all our time working, striving, earning money so that we can buy more stuff. Or we can focus on the things we love most—friends, family, and simple pleasures. I know that for many people, the economics aren't that simple; they are striving to pay the bills, not buy a lot of shiny toys. Even in those cases, there is good news: accumulation of things does not make us happy. Time with loved ones does. The best things in life really are free . . . or at least cheap.

This matter of stuff versus experience is embedded in the Jewish and Christian stories, too. The first chapter of the Bible introduces a God who creates and creates and creates. God calls each of the created things "good." Material things are good! But on the seventh day, the sabbath day, God rests. And God calls that day "holy."

Things are good, but time is holy.[3]

That night as we're finishing up dinner, I tell Robert about the study.

"I totally relate to that," he says. "It's why I 'get' Sabbath—it's time together, and that's what I value above all. And why I really have to sit and think for a long time about gifts to give people. I'm not wired to have those things come to mind easily."

"Well, and the whole Christmas season is wired toward gifts," I say. "Sure, more and more people are talking about simplicity and spending less. But tangible gifts are still the default. And what if you really love to give and receive quality time with someone . . . how does that work? How do you give *time* to a family member six states away?"

We fall silent.

The Work of Sabbath: Whatever You Want, as Long as It's Slow

My aunt Sherry fought ovarian cancer for a long time and ultimately died from it a few months before Margaret was born. She once described the experience of waiting for an oncology appointment. "I can tell who's in the waiting room with cancer and who's healthy and just dealing with an iffy test or something," she said. "The people with cancer are the ones waiting there patiently. It's kind of peaceful. It's always the healthy people who come running in or who start tapping their feet or griping to the receptionist. We're the ones whose time may be short. But they're the ones who act like it."

Her comments weren't directed at me, but I hung my head anyway. Dashing into a room, sighing at lateness—busyness is my default posture. That's why I'm drawn to Sabbath, I guess—it convicts me even as it provides an alternative way to be.

During December, we decide to get heretical with our Sabbaths: we resolve to do whatever we want on that day—no restrictions—as long as we do so completely unhurried. Chores, errands, even Christmas shopping are "legal," as long as we do them slowly.

For Robert, sabbath days are tailor-made for home brewing. Sure, he can bottle a batch of beer on a weeknight after the kids are in bed, but it's not as restorative. His enjoyment increases when he can be leisurely. Hurry sucks the joy out of a normally pleasurable activity.

Even the consumption of food can slow down on this day. Traditional Shabbat feasts are multicourse affairs. There's no need to wolf down one's food in order to get to the next commitment–there *are* no commitments on Sabbath. Robert and I try to remind the kids (and each other) to eat slowly and taste what we're consuming, even if it's a Sabbath snack of microwave popcorn.

December seems like a fun month to try an "anything goes but keep it slow" approach. Early in December I find myself with a few Christmas-related errands, and I decide to do them slowly, with an eye not for efficiency but for seeing what's going on around me.

This particular day's errands include Trader Joe's and the FedEx Kinko's store. I need supplies for some simple Christmas gifts. While at Trader Joe's I think, *There are probably groceries we need.* I contemplate a call home so Robert can confirm. Then I think, *This seems a little beyond the spirit of doing things slowly. Get through your list and enjoy yourself.* I wander up and down the aisles, noticing the people who are cheerful and those who are glum. I practice seeing the face of Christ in each person and find myself saying a silent prayer for the people I pass.

I notice who's barreling through with their carts, and I slow down even further. I notice elderly couples shopping together, carefully conferring over the right can of beans. I notice people poring over their lists with their carts obliviously parked in the middle of the aisle. On another day I might have viewed those folks as a nuisance, the thing standing between me and whatever important thing I need to do next.

Not today. These aren't obstacles. These are my neighbors. They form some of the contours of my world, even if I never exchange words with them.

When the errands are complete, I drive home. I'm not one who speeds, but I do have the heavy foot so common in Northern Virginia. Again, not today. I go the speed limit and even slightly below. I watch the last leaves fall off the trees. I count the people on cell phones amid the traffic. I sing along to the radio.

As I glance down at the bags in the passenger seat, filled with eggnog and vanilla extract, I know that I am cheating on Sabbath, plain and simple. I am letting the definitions go slack partly because that's how things will get done this month. But there are worse things I could do.

In her book *The Sabbath World,* Judith Shulevitz describes a study done at Princeton Theological Seminary on the good Samaritan, that classic story about helping others. The study sought to determine what makes a person react as the Samaritan does in the parable. The researchers performed personality tests on a group of students and then told them to report to another building, where half would give a talk about the good Samaritan story and the other half would talk about their future career as pastors.

The students were then divided further: one-third were told to hurry because the seminar had already started; one-third were told they were on time but they shouldn't dawdle; one-third were told that they had plenty of time but ought to head over there anyway.

Meanwhile, the researchers had placed a man in a nearby alley, who coughed and groaned in clear distress when each student walked by. His story was that he'd just taken some medicine for a respiratory problem and was waiting for it to kick in.

Some seminary students stopped. Others didn't. After the results were analyzed, only one variable could be used to predict whether someone would stop to help the man. It wasn't personality, and it wasn't whether they had the good Samaritan on the brain.

It was how hurried they were.

The researchers found that even those who had not stopped had seen the man, but the hurriers did not register that he needed help until well after they had passed him. "Time pressure narrowed their 'cognitive map'; as they raced by they had seen without seeing," Shulevitz writes.

It would seem, she concludes along with the researchers, that "ethics becomes a luxury as the speed of our daily lives increases."[4]

The ethic of helping others, of noticing human suffering, is not a luxury. It is nonnegotiable. So maybe I am cheating by doing errands on the Sabbath. Or maybe, by doing them slowly and intentionally, I'm getting in touch with a deeper truth of Sabbath: that our persistent drive to get things done is for naught if we ignore the humanity of those around us.

*　　*　　*

I come home from my slow errands to the smell of roasted toffee pecans cooling on the counter and homemade granola in the oven. Later the kids and I put the saucepan on the stove with a clatter, and in goes the white sugar with a *shhhhhhh,* followed by the *plunk* of the brown sugar and the thick splash of the buttermilk. My mother's pralines. In a good year, we'll make eight or nine batches to give away.

And there is joy.

I had bought a gingerbread village kit to do with the kids, but when I open the box, I see that many of the pieces are broken. I spread out the shattered triangles and rectangles and stare at them for a long time, moving the shapes around to see if anything can be salvaged. Maybe I can't make the little village church, but what about the A-frame cottage? I finally tell the kids, "You know what? We *could* figure this out. But that's more work than I want to do. So let's bag it."

Instead we make gingerbread cookies, which have the advantage of being more delicious than the prefab ginger board. We pilfer the kit for sprinkles and gumdrops, and the kids go to town. Smears of icing and sprinkles go flying. I decide that our Roomba vacuum cleaner was made for Christmas cookies.

"Poor little Roomba, having to work on the Sabbath," Caroline jokes as it rolls across the floor, bouncing off the cabinets.

That night, it's my turn to read to James before bed. Robert and I are fanatical about bedtime, partly because well-rested kids are happier kids, but mainly because we covet those precious kid-free hours in the evenings. We are not easily deterred at bedtime; stalls and pleas for "one more book" usually fall on deaf ears. But not tonight. In response to his protests, James and I read book after book, and I rest my chin on his head, rubbing it back and forth to feel his hair tickle my face.

How many times have I seen the bedtime ritual as a means to an end rather than a bliss all its own?

Too many. I vow to do better.

It won't be long before he won't fit under my chin anymore.

*　　*　　*

The next Saturday Sabbath comes with a new list of slow errands: assembling stocking stuffers and buying poinsettias for the church sanctuary. The kids stay at home with Robert and help him bottle beer—his own version of doing Sabbath slowly, since it will take him three times longer to do the job with these pint-sized helpers. As for me, I have all morning for these two tasks.

I drive to the outer reaches of the mall parking lot and pull into the first place I see, instead of circling and facing down other cars to see who'll be the first on the draw to hit the turn signal as a space opens up. I saunter toward the building and allow myself a deep breath, then cough from the exhaust of idling cars. *OK, maybe the cleansing breaths aren't such a great idea.*

That night after the kids are in bed, I ask Robert, "Remember the Saturday list?" We would get up Saturday morning and laze around for a while, then after breakfast one of us would say, "So . . . what needs to happen this weekend?" In no time we'd have a list of chores that filled the big white board in our kitchen. At this point we'd contemplate going back to sleep. The kids would scowl at it, knowing what it meant: one of us would be out of commission and unable to play, or worse, we would drag them along.

"I don't miss that," I say.

"Yes. Life seems so much nicer."

"Do you suppose that things are going to catch up to us?"

"Oh, for sure," he sighs. "I've been trying not to think about it, but we've got some projects starting to pile up. It's been a long time since we did any home improvement. The garage could use a good cleanout . . ."

"Eh, let's think about it after the holidays."

*   *   *

Christmas morning begins with a Sabbath pause. Remarkably, I am the first one awake. I lean into the quiet for a while, listening for the sound of kid-sized heels hitting the floor. Even with the shades down, I can tell it's gray and cold, but it isn't supposed to snow until the 27th, Margaret's birthday.

The kids wake up with a groggy excitement. They climb on us, all footy pajamas and hair standing on end. And then it's like mounting a sled bound for the bottom of a steep hill; it's all stockings and breakfast and presents and gasps and shards of wrapping paper and tangles of ribbons. And then the frenzy is done. We spend the rest of the day lounging, playing with our gifts, and calling family and friends. Sabbathing.

The Sabbath experiment is peeking out among the presents—we give each other gifts of time instead of things. My combined Christmas/birthday present from Robert is a few days away later in the winter to do some writing. And the kids and I give Robert an item on his bucket list: thanks to my sister in Florida, and some judicious use of frequent flyer miles, Robert will attend a space shuttle launch in the spring.

*　　*　　*

That night, after the kids are in bed, Robert and I reflect on the season over glasses of port. It was a full month, but we are not on the verge of collapse. Our slow days helped, as well as the fact that we left lots of traditional Christmas activities undone. We decorate the inside of our house, but never the outside. This makes us the Scrooges in our neighborhood, without so much as a wreath on the front door, let alone lights in the trees or inflatable Santa snow globes on the lawn. And we haven't sent Christmas cards in years.

"It was a good Christmas," Robert says.

"The best Christmas ever." I smile, recalling that my father said that every year.

He always meant it, too. Every Christmas *was* the best Christmas ever. As a child, I thought he meant they were getting better and better. Now that I'm an adult, I know that's not true. In fact, there were a few lousy Christmases in there. But what he said was still true on some level.

Dad's declaration wasn't a comparative statement. He was affirming that whatever was happening at the moment was wonderful, as good as it needed to be. The best.

Robert has heard the story a hundred times, but I tell him again about a memorable "best Christmas ever" growing up. The year after my parents separated, Christmas was a sad holiday with dual celebrations in two new, unfamiliar homes. Dad was so broke that even the little things got wrapped up—batteries, a small box of crayons—so there'd seem to be more under the tree. Yet we still managed to have a good time. On Christmas Eve we decided to have ice cream sundaes with all the trimmings. Perhaps it was a particularly warm Christmas in Houston. We put a jar of marshmallow creme into the microwave to heat it up, and the fluff expanded like a gigantic balloon. My little sister Katie, observing the seemingly magical increase, said, "We should put some money in there!"

My father, like everyone, got frustrated and disappointed. He lost his temper and wasn't always present in the moment. But "best Christmas ever" reflected the truest desire of his heart: to be content with what is.

I wish he were still here; he died several years ago. But some of his yearnings live on in me. Learning to be content in time has been what the Sabbath experiment is all about.

6

January

Holy is the place I stand
To give whatever small good I can
The empty page, the open book
Redemption everywhere I look
Unknowingly we slow our pace
In the shade of unexpected grace
With grateful smiles and sad lament
As holy as a day is spent
And morning light sings "providence"
As holy as a day is spent.

—CARRIE NEWCOMER[1]

"Well, Robert," I say toward the end of December, "we're a third of the way through the Sabbath year, and it's New Year's resolution time. What do you think? Do we keep going?"

"Oh yeah. Definitely."

* * *

For many Jews who observe the Sabbath, the day begins at sundown Friday night with the lighting of candles and blessings. Ours begins in the dreamy haze of a Saturday morning.

We spend Friday nights finishing up work tasks or cramming chores before the next day's Sabbath begins—collecting stray glasses around the house for one last load of dishes, scooping up plush animals and tossing them into the stuffed toy basket, answering a few e-mails before the weekend. If we're feeling burned out, though, we declare Friday night a Sabbath too, errant plush animals be damned.

As we tuck our children into bed that night, we assure them that tomorrow is Sabbath and they can sleep as long as they want. "We don't have to go *anywhere*," they sigh, and we kiss their foreheads. I feel a pang of guilt. I love that the day is something they anticipate, but it's hard not to see their relief as a commentary on the rest of our days, which involves a lot of "going anywhere."

The next morning, Sabbath comes to us . . . not with the strike of a match and a prayer in Hebrew, but with the creep of small feet.

First there's a creak of a bed or bunk bed ladder. A thump of feet hitting the floor.

Then there's the quick squeak of a door and a considerate reclosing of it, in case the other inhabitant of the room wants to sleep longer.

Then comes the quiet shuffle down the hall and, in the case of the two younger ones, a folding into our bed. Caroline often curls up in the chair in our room, usually with a book, and waits for her parents to come slowly to life. It is not all that late—barely 7 a.m.—but it's later, and gentler, than our weekly routine. Words are few and far between. Sabbath doesn't start so much as emerge.

Sometimes, there is a whisper in my ear: "Can we get ourselves a snack downstairs?" (You mean, can you do something independently that doesn't require me to get out of bed yet? A thousand times yes, my dear.)

During the week, we are awake well before our children, showered and ready for action. I've often done an hour of work by the time they wake, and Robert has left the house without seeing them at all. But on the Sabbath, our children are the ones who inaugurate the day for us.

*   *   *

Several months into the experiment, we are starting to crave Sabbath time. A dinnertime report of a hectic day or a burgeoning to-do list prompts the reply, "Three days to Sabbath." The character of the Sabbath is changing too as the winter sets in. There aren't as many field trips as in the fall. We're not venturing out. Our adventures take place in the house: art projects, silly games, cooking. I remember my ambivalence about engaging in family Sabbath activities that require other people to work. Sabbath in the home feels like it has more integrity—granted, the stores are still open and the system is still alive, but we're not taking part in it. We're off the consumer grid.

Unfortunately, any holy glow of Sabbath is elusive. The token system for television watching continues to keep the whining at bay, but our children don't have the same interests at ages seven, five, and three. There are times when they play together so well—watching them is a thing of divine (frequently hilarious) beauty, right in the middle of our suburban tract home with the dusty baseboards. Other times it's a chore to help them find things to do. Caroline has only recently started to read books that are advanced enough to hold her interest. At the same time, she's outgrowing many of the toys that litter our family room.

As a prekindergartner, Margaret doesn't read. She's still neck-deep in princess play, but her older and younger siblings aren't interested in being Jaq and Gus to her Cinderella. And James, barely three, will play for hours with his trains, but he still needs help building the track and weeps piteously when the bridge piece topples off, which it does with annoying regularity.

Nonsabbath time is so structured for children—with school, playdates (even calling them "playdates" suggests an appointment rather than a relaxed time of play), activities, trips to the library, preschool, errands, working parents, and daycare—that children don't know what to do with an abundance of time. Sabbath feels like a foreign country—the food is great and the customs are appealing, but it's just *different.* Our family is less programmed than many. But until we started this project, our children only rarely had an entire day to do as they wished.

There are fights, whining, and jockeying for parents' attention. There are times when a kid seems desperate for Mommy or Daddy— they *need* one of us and don't want to share. When we go for a walk, Caroline will want to hold my hand—but only if neither of her siblings is holding the other one. They argue over whose activity will come first. When we suggest an alternate activity for the kid who doesn't get her way, the first child instantly decides *that's* what *she* wants to do instead.

After four months, I now understand why I didn't find a lot of books about Sabbath written by parents of young children.

This is a typical scene. I look around, see everyone engaged in an activity, and pick up a book or magazine.

"Mommy?" It's Margaret. "Will you get down the doll bin for me?"

I do and go back to reading.

A few minutes later, from the hallway bathroom, a plaintive request from the boy: "Can you wipe me?"

I go back to reading. It takes me a minute to find my place.

Soon I must intervene because Kid A is hitting Kid B.

Back to reading.

"Can I have a snack?"

"No, Caroline, it's not snack time yet."

Meanwhile, I've read two paragraphs.

These disruptions are typical kid things and have nothing to do with Sabbath. But they are a reminder that kids don't care about set-apart time in the same way we do. Arguing, negotiating, fits of independence followed by clinginess to the parental home base—these are developmental stages, the vital work of childhood, however exasperating they often are. And they do not cease when Sabbath starts. These little people are growing, always growing. Sabbath may mean "stop" in Hebrew, but in the language of our household, it will never fully mean that. Kids do not stop; they are ever learning how to be the people they're meant to be, which requires a lot of acting out who they *aren't* meant to be.

Till, is it unreasonable for grownups to have a *tiny* bit of Sabbath carved out for grown-ups to savor without interruption? I reject the idea that parents must delay and defer all their own needs for the sake of their children. One of my wisest friends once told me, "A great gift you can give your child is the knowledge that you, too, have limits." I would like to read for more than 2.8 minutes without interruption. Robert has similar issues—he has less time during the week with the kids than I do, so Sabbath becomes an important time to reconnect with them. At the same time, he's an introvert in an extroverted job, so he needs time to restore.

We consider setting some kind of routine with the Sabbath, breaking it up into "apart time" and "together time." But ultimately we bag the idea. We hate to slice and dice the day even more—our life is choppy enough the rest of the week. So we let the issue go and decide to keep an eye on it. I suspect this push and pull between togetherness and separateness will always be a tension on the Sabbath.

Sabbath Hack: Kid Lists and the Parking Lot

We have stumbled upon another Sabbath hack: lists. David Allen, an organizational guru and author of the book *Getting Things Done*, talks about lists as one of the most powerful personal tools we have.[2] I am a connoisseur of to-do lists. During the week I will sometimes build a monster to-do list, broken down into small chunks, and challenge myself to get through as much as I can in one day.

Lists can also be draining. Our old weekend to-do lists, full of needful tasks, overwhelmed us—there's no way we could get it all done. These lists also pelted us with guilt—*How can we take time to play? We haven't even made a dent in our list!* We don't make those lists anymore. Instead we decide on the few things we have time for and let the rest go.

But Sabbath lists? Those are fun. We fill pages or white boards with the frivolous things we don't have space for during the week. The list becomes a menu of scrumptious options.

Lists are especially important for our kids, who are learning how to entertain themselves and need guidance. When a child says she is bored, I will refer her to the "kid list" to see what sparks an interest. A handmade card for a grandparent? A game of UNO? Watercoloring? The suggestions don't always ignite, of course. But they often provide enough of a reset to short-circuit the "I'm bored" loop.

We also use lists as a parking lot for ideas. We often think of something on the Sabbath that we should take care of, and rather than expend any mental energy trying to remember it—or, more likely for me, actually doing it—we will "park it" in the parking lot. After Sabbath ends, we clean out the parking lot.

Lists may seem like the anti-Sabbath activity. They are so linear, so methodically minded. But I see this kind of list-making as an act of prayer. The list of Sabbath delights is a prayer of thanksgiving to a God who delights in the rhythms of work and play, of effort and rest. And the parking lot is a place to put good intentions and plans, knowing that they will be held in holy space until the appointed time.

*   *   *

It's Monday, piano day. When the kids and I pick up Caroline from her lesson, her teacher tells us, "She really has a beautiful voice—she's always singing along while she plays. Have you thought about putting her in a choir?" I have. Caroline not only sings but experiments—making up melodies, picking out harmonies. Robert and I have sung in choirs our whole lives, and I even did a couple of musicals as a college student.

We don't have a children's choir at our church, so that evening I click around Google to see what's out there. There is a children's community choir in our area, and what luck! They are accepting additional singers right now. They even meet on Mondays; rehearsals would be an easy, unhurried drive from our piano teacher's house. It seems perfect.

I broach the subject to Caroline. "No. Definitely not."

"But you love to sing."

"I don't want to."

"Are you sure? Why?"

"I just don't want to. It's too much on Mondays."

She has a point. Our Mondays feel hectic right now, despite being my day off. Caroline gets home from school and all she wants to do is play and unwind. Meanwhile the younger two have had an entire morning to get into the relaxation groove, and the last thing *they* want to do is get in the car to drop off Caroline at piano practice, even though I try to make the most of the time she's at her lesson. (Even a mandatory trip to the pet store can be fun if we wander the store, visiting all the mice, corn snakes, and ferrets.)

Getting out the door for piano is a trial and somehow harder than other departures during the week. The Monday after the choir conversation, I lose my cool. James is shrieking over the indignity of putting on his shoes, and on impulse, I slap him on the thigh. I finally wrestle him into the car as he continues to whimper. I grip the wheel and breathe, appalled at myself. Then I hear Caroline from the backseat: "It's a good thing we're not doing the choir thing or it would be even worse."

Later that week the e-mail arrives about winter swim—Caroline's summer team gets together once a week during the off-season for an informal practice. It doesn't conflict with our usual Sabbath. But it's yet another thing. And it will disrupt Sunday night, which has become almost as sacred as Sabbath: we eat pizza in the basement and watch a show together. We decide not to sign up.

In the space of one week, we've received two opportunities to step up our kid's activities. How much is too much? Robert tells me that "everyone" in his office has children in foreign language classes. This information is a data point from him, not a suggestion, but it pulls on me because I know that early exposure to language means that children can learn a language more easily later. Some brain things that don't get turned on when they are young don't get fully turned on.

But play is the work of childhood. Caroline is still young enough that I don't want to shortchange that most basic activity. She will grow up and have appointments soon enough. Better for her to day-dream, doodle, and ride slow looping circles on her bike while she still can.

As digital culture becomes increasingly prevalent, I read more and more articles about the impact of this technology and pace of information on our brains, our health, and our ability to think creatively. I don't know whether the world is moving faster than it used to, but it certainly feels like it. I don't know what these shifts mean for our children.

Maybe Sabbath is a vaccination against the breakneck speed of life. I have hope that our family's adherence to a different way, a way that includes a gentler rhythm to the week, means that Caroline and her siblings will have access to a well of creativity and thoughtfulness that will serve them well. I hope that Sabbath will also give them a spiritual foundation, a grasp of simplicity, and a more expansive view of time, whatever faith they might happen to follow as an adult.

But maybe it won't. Maybe we need to embrace the insanity, plunge into the busyness and make friends with it. A friend of mine calls the child-raising phase of life "the crazy years." Maybe it's OK to accept that and to plunge into these activities—all of them.

In my better moments, I think we can't go wrong whatever we choose. I feel grateful that we have these decisions to make and so many opportunities available. Art, music, sports—these are the things that give texture and joy to life.

In my lesser moments, I feel torn. If we restrict what they do, they miss out on great opportunities. If we go in more, a bit of childhood gets lost in the shuffle. There's the potential for regret either way I go.

* * *

If it's winter in our house, chances are good that someone's sick. This time it's Caroline, who comes down with the flu three days before Margaret's fifth birthday party. The poor birthday girl has already had to wait; her birthday is in late December, when a lot of folks are out of town or focused on family stuff. We'd decided to have a "pretend slumber party" in mid-January, in which kids will wear PJs and bring sleeping bags and stuffed animals but go home at bedtime.

We have a decision to make: Do we postpone? Do we go ahead with the party somewhere else? Or do we have it at our house as planned and sequester the sick kid offsite? Even if we could find a place for Caroline to be, would people still let their kids come? I've been attacking all the counters, doorknobs, and faucets with Lysol, but I'm not that confident in my germ-eradicating skills.

I do what many modern parents do when confronted with a dilemma. I take it to Facebook, and the advice pours in:

"Postpone, so Caroline can attend her own sister's party."

"Have it as planned. Don't worry about trying to sequester Caroline. Everybody's got germs floating around these days. It's January." (Apparently I have some devious friends.)

"Go ahead on Saturday; just have it somewhere other than your house." (I do a little calling around—I can't get the recreation center people to call me back, and I can't stand Chuck E. Cheese, which my brother calls the "casino for kids.")

I really like the last option—having it somewhere else. As a recovering control freak, I've got to grab my spontaneity where I can get it. Moving to plan B seems like a good exercise in being flexible and going with the flow. And if we reschedule, who's to say that Margaret won't be sick on the new date? There are no guarantees, especially in our home, with its revolving door of viruses. But something keeps needling me.

I try to explain it to Robert. "I feel like Sabbath is . . . I don't know . . . it's trying to speak to us."

"What do you mean?" (I suspect that he knows what I mean but has decided not to let me off the hook for such a flaky comment. We're not the type of people to be addressed by abstract concepts of time, after all.)

"Well, this year is about more than taking Sabbath once a week. It's been about approaching time in a completely different way. To not be anxious and frantic in how we spend our days. So why rush around for the sake of a new plan?"

He looks skeptical.

"And what's more important?" I continue. "Having the experience that Margaret really wants to have, with her sister there, whom she adores . . . or doing something this weekend just because that's what we planned? Do *we* run our lives or does the calendar?"

"Are you kidding? We postpone this and Margaret is going to freak out."

"Yeah, you're right," I say, deflated after my rousing Sabbath-is-talking-to-us speech.

"Hey," he says after a minute. "What about Queen for a Day?" He's referring to a thing we've done a couple of times when we let our kids call all the shots for an entire day. Perhaps being Queen for a Day might cushion the disappointment.

Ultimately, we decide to postpone the party and let Margaret be queen of Sabbath that weekend. (I have actually run across references to "Queen Sabbath" in various books and articles, in connection with the Jewish Sabbath. Sounds beautiful, but I worry we are mucking up a perfectly good religious tradition by electing our own queen.)

And the queen is devastated: "I've already had to wait!" she shrieks. She goes through all the stages of grief in rapid succession—anger, bargaining, and finally, an acceptance that becomes less and less grudging the more she thinks about Queen for a Day.

I remember the first time I heard the expression "found time," after someone canceled a meeting at the last minute that I'd planned to attend. It is a delicious image, found time. There it is, gleaming like a penny on the ground.

What do we do with our found time?

We have Sabbath, of course, Margaret-style: lots of games, dolls, movies, and the promise of a party in a couple of weeks. Meanwhile, Caroline's fever breaks.

*   *   *

It's early evening on a Sabbath when I learn about Tucson. A congresswoman and several people have been shot, some fatally. I get the news through Facebook, which I've logged into at an idle moment. Through the tributes, links, laments, and predictable anti- and progun sentiments that get voiced during events like this, I piece together what has happened. As I click from article to article, I feel strange that while I was in my own little world, terrible events were transpiring.

I think back to the 9/11 attacks, which happened while I was in seminary in Atlanta. We were told about the planes hitting the Twin Towers in the middle of Hebrew class. Afterward, someone wheeled a television into the hallway, and many of us saw the towers fall. These days, during the course of my life, I'm rarely very far from e-mail, the radio, or an Internet newsfeed. So to have a tragedy like Tucson unfold over several hours while I was blithely knitting a Harry Potter scarf for Caroline is bizarre.

It's bizarre but also liberating. I'm heartbroken for the victims and their families, but after a while, I decide to turn off the computer. All year, Sabbath has been reminding me that I am not indispensable. I can do nothing to change what has happened. I cannot alter the trajectory of this story as it moves forward either, and sitting at my computer, combing news sites for additional bits of information about the shooter, does nobody any good.

The world has gotten a lot smaller, thanks in part to the 24-7 news cycle. I am grateful for many aspects of our hyperconnected world. But I'm feeling a little frayed around the edges from all this togetherness. Within hours, we know all kinds of details about the gunman, Jared Lee Loughner, and the theories spread like wildfire as to his motives and alleged political leanings. Many of these theories will turn out to be false, but by then it will be too late. These snatches of information, fed to a hungry public, will only confirm what people are already inclined to believe. We hear what we want to hear. We become more entrenched, stony, and immobile in our views. We become more polarized.

Time will tell us what we need to know. I believe this. Sabbath is so much deeper than a weekly rest and renewal. Sabbath fosters perspective and clarity. Through Sabbath, perhaps, we can learn the difference between urgent and important. We can learn that reading or commenting on news articles is not the same thing as working for the healing of the world—it only gives us the illusion of doing something useful.

As I watch my laptop screen flash into darkness, I feel a sense of relief. Yes, the world falls apart, even on the Sabbath. Tomorrow I will do my small part to put it back together again, whatever that might be. But today, taking this time to cherish family, self, and God is the most faithful way I can think of to begin.

*　*　*

It is Wednesday, a work-at-home day. I am tucked into the old armchair in my bedroom, marching through the to-do list, typing e-mails, letting my sermon simmer in the mental Crock-Pot, when my pocket buzzes. It is a text message from a friend: "We wanted to see if you were on your way to the clergy group." *Oh, crap!* I glance at the clock and calculate: if I leave right now, I'll barely make it there before the meeting ends. I've stood up eight treasured companions on this ministry journey. A sliver of guilt and confusion slices through me—I don't miss meetings. Occasionally I will bow out of one, and I'll even do it for vague reasons of mental health. But I can't recall actually *forgetting* one. What is that about?

Two days later, I'm typing a newsletter article, under deadline, when the phone rings. It is a friend of mine. Her voice is kind and tentative: "Were we going to have tea today?"

I look at the clock, sigh, and say, "You're actually one of many people I've stood up this week. Does it make you feel better that you're in such abundant company?"

Again I ask, what is this about?

I blame the Sabbath—or more accurately, my misuse of it. I realize that I've been using the day for my own ends: *I can go ninety miles an hour the rest of the time,* I tell myself, *because I stop once a week. Work hard, crash hard.* But it doesn't work that way. Sabbath isn't simply a once-a-week thing; it's meant to change how I look at the rest of my life.

This week, something in my body wanted to be home instead of at those meetings. We're now in the middle stages of this yearlong Sabbath journey, and a hunger has been awakened. The more Sabbath I have, the more I want. This scares me, frankly.

Sabbath is no longer a day or even a mind-set—it's becoming a force, a living entity in our lives. Or perhaps that living entity is God, speaking to me through the language of Sabbath, a language that isn't always soft and nice. This week, I hear the words of a gangster, all shadowy in his trench coat and fedora: "This is a nice little Type-A life you've got here. Be a shame if something happened to it."

That night I say to Robert, "Honey, make sure I make it to church on Sunday, OK? I suddenly don't trust myself."

Robert laughs, "Yeah, what's going on with you this week? This is not like you."

"I think it's Sabbath's fault," I quip.

He is the voice of rationality: "Or you need some better remind-ers in Google Calendar."

"OK, fine. I'll go with 'both.'"

It's also the winter working on me, I think. This time of year, I feel an urge to hibernate. I curl up in chairs or bring a book to bed, huddling under blankets. The cold weather affects all of us. Maybe in the spring we will venture beyond our family room for Sabbath, taking long walks and bike rides. But for now, our whole family seems content not to take up too much space.

I will try to trust this impulse. I imagine that we are like the daf-fodil and tulip bulbs crouching in the earth with hunched shoulders, looking for all the world like a lump of not-much-of-anything but secretly full of possibility. Ready to stretch up and out at the first sign of spring. But not until a moment before.

Over the weekend Margaret takes a short out-of-town trip with my mother. She is glad to see all of us when she returns and seems much older than five after this big-kid privilege with her MaDear. But after visiting extended family in Texas for several days, she is overloaded.

I later find her in our living room, a place that doesn't get much use except for Caroline's piano playing. It's where I put kids when they need a time-out. I put myself there too, regularly and for the same reason. Margaret has built a small nest in one of the chairs, complete with pillow walls, umbrella roof, and a sign that her sister helped her write: "Do Not Disterb." I peek in and see her there, her favorite books in a pile at her feet.

I know the feeling, my child. Honor that feeling. Go with it.

*   *   *

Margaret's birthday party finally comes, and it is a mix of joy-ful screeches, musical sleeping bags, and smears of icing from the cupcake decorating. It's everything she hoped it would be. The next day, Sunday, is our Sabbath. I've recently finished reading the first Harry Potter book with the girls, which means we're ready to watch the movie. The girls rests their heads on my shoulders as they take it all in; they are enchanted and overcome by what they see. We make popcorn the old-fashioned way, on the stove, since we're out of the microwaveable bags. Stovetop popcorn feels more Sabbath-y than the two-minute microwave variety, and it tastes better, too.

James wanders in and out of the basement from time to time but spends much of the time upstairs with Robert, especially during the scary parts of the movie.

When the video is over, we come upstairs to see what the menfolk have been doing. Robert is coming in from the deck and closes the sliding door behind him.

"I built a rack for our firewood!"

"Um, wow! In the time it took us to watch a movie?"

"Yep, come see."

He shows me his handiwork, a simple but sturdy thing made out of some discarded planks we had piled up on the side of our house from an old home improvement project.

Building a rack for firewood seems like a lot of work to me for a Sabbath, but we don't talk about it until after the kids are in bed.

"That was good for my mental health," he says as he opens one of his homebrews.

"I'm glad you think so. I was feeling bad that you didn't exactly get a Sabbath."

"Oh, but I did. Projects like that are actually kinda restful. Especially because I was able to use stuff on hand. If it had been more complicated, it wouldn't have felt that way. I mean, I didn't even have to go to the hardware store!"

The Work of Sabbath: Novelty

Robert's experience with the firewood rack is a great example of bringing oneself back into balance, a Sabbath approach we stumbled on a few months ago. It is a physical activity that requires manual labor, creativity, and problem solving. But the project goes beyond that. The firewood rack also demonstrates the power of novelty as a source of energy and renewal in people's lives. Our days are made up of routines, and an impromptu construction project, however small, is a welcome break from the regular rhythm of work (commutes, meetings, e-mail) and home life (cooking, bathing kids, paying bills). Sabbath itself is a break from the routine; shouldn't the things we do on that day reflect that novelty?

Studies have shown that pursuing an unfamiliar or nonroutine task can increase satisfaction, and Gretchen Rubin writes in her book *The Happiness Project* that novelty is one of the keys to happiness. Breaking out of the humdrum of the everyday actually produces physiological changes in the body, which stimulate the pleasure centers in the brain.[3]

The Sabbath is about more than feeling happy, of course. Emotions can be fleeting, and we're after something deeper in our year of Sabbath than a warm fuzzy feeling. But there's a spiritual dimension to this novelty stuff. A church I used to serve borrows from the prophet Isaiah (chap. 43:18) in its motto: "Behold, I am doing a new thing!" It is a constant reminder for the congregation that God calls us to move beyond "the way we've always done it."

There are deep patterns and rhythms in the biblical story, but there are also countless holy surprises that disrupt our expectations: a pregnancy for the woman thought to be barren, a giant struck down by a young boy's slingshot, a valley of dry bones rattling to life. And Jesus' ministry was anything but routine; he preached and healed and taught in countless astonishing ways. We can make a lot of competing claims about Jesus, but we can say one thing with certainty: he was never boring. The Sabbath that God calls us to observe shouldn't be either.

7

February

Every swept floor invites another sweeping, every child bathed invites another bathing. When all life moves in such cycles, what is ever finished? The sun goes 'round, the moon goes 'round, the tides and seasons go 'round, people are born and die, and when are we finished? If we refuse rest until we are finished, we will never rest until we die.

—WAYNE MULLER[1]

It's Sunday afternoon and the children are watching the sky. It's tantalizingly bleak, heavy with gray clouds, but . . . no snow.

"It's happening again. I don't get it," I say to Robert. "Eastern Pennsylvania is getting socked. Areas all around us are getting inches. But here? Nothing."

"It's a snow bubble," he says.

People in our area (and our own household) are a little weirded out by the lack of snow this year. We've had a couple of flurries but nothing substantial. Meanwhile areas all around us have gotten hit by snowstorms.

Not everyone loves snow, and it comes with serious downsides—dangerously cold temperatures and occasional power outages, not to mention the impact on the elderly who live alone or people without homes or adequate heating in those homes. But it also gives our area a pause. The DC region seems to depend on one or two moderate snowstorms to release the pressure valve. Schools and the federal government close, and many businesses follow suit. Snow provides a spiritual reset in this fast-paced culture.

The previous year we had a huge snowstorm, dubbed Snowpocalypse or Snowmaggedon depending on the news network. More than two feet of snow fell and the area shut down for the better part of a week. Snowpocalypse was a lot of work, but it also blanketed the area with peace. As a friend wrote on Facebook, "I wonder if snow days are God's way of saying, 'If you won't take a Sabbath for yourself, I'm going to enforce one with this cold manna-type stuff. Have some cocoa and relax, will ya?'"

I love the story she's talking about: God provides the starving people of Israel with bread in the wilderness, a "fine flaky substance, as fine as frost on the ground" (Ex. 16:14). I'm struck with how improbable the story is. *Manna* in Hebrew literally means "what is it?" and I laugh to think about the Israelites looking confused but delighted as the desert sky rains breadcrumbs. (As a child, I always pictured it looking and tasting like yellow cake.) Then I picture them scooping up handfuls of the flaky stuff and throwing it at each other . . . a manna-ball fight. Followed by a manna-man-building contest. Then manna angels.

God provides in such eccentric ways. Bread from heaven that feeds a people. A day of rest, cold and crystalline.

Having grown up in Texas and made exactly one snowman as a child—a Yoda-sized thing studded with bits of grass since the dusting of snow was so slight—I can't get enough of the stuff. I miss it this year, because who doesn't love a bonus Sabbath? But I'm also glad that we have set aside Sabbath each week. Our calendar will remind us to pause and rest, even if the sky stays clear. We're never more than six days away from a spiritual snow day.

*   *   *

Sometimes, the so-called mommy wars are waged over breast-feeding versus bottle, or crib versus family bed. Sometimes, they begin over baked goods.

It all starts in a very silly way. I post an offhand comment on Facebook gushing about the glory that is Trader Joe's pumpkin bread mix. It has provided spicy goodness, fresh from the oven, on many a sabbath day this winter (not to mention random Tuesdays and Fridays). You only need an egg and some oil, as opposed to canned pumpkin and a bevy of spices I don't often have on hand.

A friend responds dismissively, asking why someone would need a *mix* in order to make pumpkin bread, which after all is *so easy.*

I feel an angry flash of *Who asked you?* followed by the briefest tremor of shame—*if I really loved my family, I'd make them something homemade.* Then I decide not to take the bait. To each her own, right? I celebrate pumpkin bread in all its forms. Later though, I feel unsettled. Our kitchen feeds five people several times a day. What's wrong with using a mix when the result is just as good?

"I don't know," I tell Robert later. "It's so stupid, but it hit a nerve. I mean, I agree with her. I *do* value the handmade and homemade. We live in such a cut-corners society. But the thing is . . . it's kinda fun when you find a good shortcut"

"Maximum impact, minimum effort," he nods, sharing his father's famous approach to cooking. Both Robert and my father-in-law are whizzes in the kitchen.

"Exactly! Do I have to be judged for my approach to *breakfast food?* Come on."

"Hey, it's pumpkin bread. Don't overthink it."

While I'm glad he doesn't share my angst, I know that the issue of domestic chores runs down gender lines. There are entire industries devoted to helping people save time and offload household tasks. At the same time, there's still a view of motherhood that values the loving hands at home. Working mothers in particular can feel caught between the necessity of delegating certain domestic chores and a feeling of guilt because they "should" do those things.

Sabbath is not making this conflict easier; it's complicating it. On the one hand, it's robbing me of an entire day of labor each week, which makes the time-savers feel necessary. On the other hand, the unhurried nature of Sabbath makes me want to slow down for the rest of the week and *not* cut corners. It's a curious irony: Sabbath reminds me that I don't have to be Supermom, but it heightens my desire to try.

I feel this tension as I consider what it means to be a "host," to provide gracious space not only for guests who might enter our home but also our own family. The biblical practice is *hospitality,* a word that's almost as old-fashioned and foreign to our ears as Sabbath. Yet hospitality is a deep and vital spiritual practice in the Jewish and Christian faiths and in other traditions. Scripture is rife with examples of people welcoming friends and travelers alike into their homes and lives. We are called to greet strangers as friends and to share abundantly with them, and Jesus offers harsh words for people who fail to show adequate hospitality.

In recent decades, the picture has been complicated by Martha Stewart's magazine and other resources that equate hospitality with handmade place cards and expensive flatware. These magazines miss the point of hospitality. I've sat at immaculate dinner tables and felt like an unwelcome afterthought, and I've been served wine in a plastic cup and felt like a treasured guest. A spirit of hospitality cannot be faked.

Still, there's no denying that, all things being equal, a spirit of hospitality comes through when someone has taken the time to prepare for the presence of another—and not in a slapdash way.

Much of my life feels slapdash. I love finding ways to save time—a new route to the church, a quicker way to put away the groceries. (If I were a superhero, efficiency would be my power. Sad but true.) Sabbath has forced me to face the shadow side. Why am I trying to save all this time? For what purpose do I hurry? So that I can do more and more stuff? To feel useful and efficient?

Sabbath-keeping makes the idea of saving time feel ridiculous . . . like we're trying to cheat at a game, but the joke's on us: this game's rules are unbendable. Maybe Sabbath is my kryptonite.

Valentine's Day is coming up, and in the past, I have rolled my eyes at the over-the-top machinations of a few of my fellow mothers. I've been preparing for our church's annual meeting and training for church officers, as well as juggling a writing deadline or two. I won't be putting together bags of goodies for the other kids at James's daycare, yet other mothers will. We don't have Margaret draw an individual picture on each of the valentines she's expected to give to her preschool class—her signed name is all we can manage.

This year we wait until the last minute to buy Valentine cards for Caroline's class exchange, only to find that the grocery store is out. We find some printable cards on the Internet, which we have to print on the black and white printer because our ancient color printer is out of ink. *I kinda suck at this,* I tell myself, though I try to be cheerful about my V-day ineptitude as we cut out black-and-white valentines on plain white copy paper.

I shouldn't roll my eyes at the other moms' observance of Valentine's Day. They are showing their love in tangible, homemade ways—the very issue that started this whole train of thought in the first place. They can make pumpkin bread their way. I'll make it mine.

*   *   *

Valentine's weekend is also Caroline's eighth birthday, and we decide to celebrate on a Saturday. We wonder if there's a way to do it Sabbathly. I've been MaryAnn the Cruise Director many times during our kids' birthday parties, most recently at Margaret's the previous month. I end up calling on my skills as a former church youth director: Games! Silliness! Sugar! There's an art to reading the crowd, knowing when to jack up the energy and when to chill them out with quieter games. But this year we consider some alternatives.

With Caroline's enthusiastic approval, we invite her two best friends to her favorite "fancy" lunch place. Then Robert and James go home for naptime while I take the girls to paint pottery at a pottery shop. Couples on dates paint at small tables nearby as Caroline's friends open up about families, school stuff and the latest tween pop star. It's lovely, sweet, and holy in its own way. I tell them the story of Caroline's birth, with the birthday girl's permission and prompting. The girls giggle as I describe her first poop as a newborn, a voluminous sticky mess that I was happy to watch Robert clean up as I rested in the hospital bed nearby.

I have chosen a simple bowl for my project and paint a series of circles around the rim. I am mesmerized at the way the paint soaks into the pottery, like it's thirsty for color. I know the feeling. Later we head back to our house for cake. Caroline, our reserved child who can get overwhelmed with crowds, has a great time . . . and I feel like I've stumbled on another secret of life: a houseful of kids is a fantastic thing, but hushed, laughing conversations over pottery are beautiful, too.

*   *   *

"You can make a longhouse, a teepee, or a pueblo," I tell Caroline, skimming the project assignment.

"Pueblo. Definitely pueblo. It's the hardest one."

"OK, well, have you thought about how you want to do this? What kind of materials you might need? Let's break it down into parts." The ghosts of childhood projects are lurking around me, memories of waiting until the last minute only to realize I didn't have the right materials to get it done. Sometimes my parents would bail me out; sometimes I'd have to make do with what was available, usually with ruinous results.

She looks over my shoulder at the assignment. "I think maybe a piece of cardboard for the base, and some clay, and some wood or toothpicks to make the cross pieces."

I set her to the task of writing down the different steps of the project. I am artistically challenged—the ceramic bowl at the pottery shop tested my limits—but helping her with a project plan is where I shine. I also think about the timing: Saturday is Sabbath. If I don't work on the Sabbath, then she shouldn't either. This is the first time that Caroline has had schoolwork that might impact our observance of the Sabbath. It's the first, but it won't be the last, I know: Someday, teenage Caroline (and teenage Margaret and James) will have projects, choir concerts, speech tournaments, and heaven knows what. What then?

Several years ago, the church I served made a big push to encourage Sabbath-taking. Very few families of teenagers participated, and I could see why. Only one family with teens made it through the eight-week experiment. I think they succeeded because they set the bar low: a weekly family walk with the dog. It was all the Sabbath they could manage between drama, cello, and ballet. Other families appreciated the project because it got them thinking about Sabbath. "But," they would say, "*thinking* is as far as we got. We couldn't figure out how to do it." I wondered at the time if their words would be mine someday.

We help Caroline get ready for her pueblo project the rest of the week—buying clay and cutting the cardboard base. Saturday we take Sabbath as usual, which means Sunday is pueblo day. Caroline spends more than an hour shaping the clay into round, flat pieces that she affixes to the milk carton we've salvaged from the school cafeteria. We're in good shape—Monday she'll finish up the details and Tuesday she'll turn it in. Project finished and Sabbath protected.

Monday morning we wake up to discover what craftier types could have told us: clay shrinks when it dries, and the milk carton is clearly peeking out between the small brown chips of dried clay. I had planned to work on Monday, but I shuffle my schedule and head to the craft store for a different kind of clay. We also need paint, since the new clay isn't brown. When Caroline gets home she hurries to redo the project before piano. That night she brushes some paint on the pueblo and we hope for the best. There's no time for this not to work.

It's all right in the end. But a thought nags: *If you hadn't worried so much about Sabbath, you wouldn't have had to rush.* "The Sabbath seems designed to make life as inconvenient as possible," writes Judith Shulevitz, a sentiment I've recalled repeatedly this year.[2] Sometimes, I can see a holy purpose in the inconvenience. Other times, I'm just annoyed in the checkout line of the craft store.

*   *   *

I look at my work calendar for the next month, really look at it, and my heart sinks. For the next several weeks, I have something scheduled on each and every Saturday.

"What are we going to do?" I ask Robert the next time we have a moment to sit down and talk.

"Let's take it a week at a time," he suggests. "If it's only a morning thing, we can do Saturday afternoon Sabbath together. Especially if you've got something Sunday after church. Or the kids and I can get started without you."

Each of these scheduled events is important in its own way. I've made a commitment to them. But we've committed to Sabbath too, and I'm not willing to suspend our practice of it. Somehow, they will have to coexist. After all, I remind myself, our year of Sabbath is an experiment in what it's like to stop and to see how that stopping transforms our lives. It doesn't violate the spirit of that experiment to shift things as needed. I remind myself of the work of Sabbath: boundaries are like the coastline, not a brick wall.

I spend the next Saturday at a training session with several people from the church. It is energizing and exciting, with lots of ideas shared. Robert and the kids go to the Building Museum downtown while I am away. I receive texted photos throughout the day of the kids messing with Legos and dashing along the long marble floors of the museum's cavernous atrium. I get home at 5 p.m. exhausted but determined to take a personal Sabbath tomorrow the moment I get home from church.

The next day after worship I have a meeting with our congregation's book group. I leave church around 2:30, tired but happy. We always have great discussions; I love a group that's willing to actually disagree over a book. I'm ready for Sabbath though; it's been a long, strenuous, fruitful weekend. Time to unplug. *The twenty-minute drive home is all that stands between me and Sabbath,* I think with a joy that almost frightens me in its intensity. Then comes the buzz in my purse. Robert: "The kids and I went to the store, but I forgot milk for tonight. Could you please? They are melting down right now."

Nothing cataclysmic happens. I don't curse at the top of my lungs or drive home and passive-aggressively pretend I didn't get the message. I just go to the grocery store and stand in line and think, *Make that "a twenty-minute drive and a gallon of milk." No problem.*

It's only after I get home that the peculiar thing happens: I keep going. I don't rest. I decide the kitchen needs cleaning. I check e-mail and write a blog post. I pay some bills. It feels like an out-of-body experience. I'd wanted Sabbath so badly, and here I was, sabotaging it for no good reason.

Sometimes kids will get so tired that they can't sleep. Is that what happened to me? Am I so tired after the weekend that even *stopping* takes too much mental energy? Or is it a weird perfectionist thing? I can't have a full day of Sabbath so I won't take any Sabbath at all? Whatever the reason, I feel like the apostle Paul, who wrote in bewilderment at his own behavior: "I do not understand my own actions. For I do not do what I want, but I do the very thing I hate" (Rom. 7:15).

"I can't make heads or tails of this," I tell Robert later, who'd been steering clear of the White Tornado all afternoon.

"Oh hey!" he says. "I bet it was the . . . what's it called again? Oh yeah: the extinction burst."

"The what?"

"I ran across a blog the other day. Basically, your brain is wired to get rewards for certain behaviors. You eat fatty foods, your pleasure centers get triggered."

"Got it so far," I reply. *All too well,* I think.

"So when you go on a diet, those rewards don't get triggered. But rather than getting switched off, your brain will do anything and everything to turn the old habit back on again."

"So you end up going off your diet, not just a little but a lot."

"Right, it's like this last-ditch burst of activity. Like an alcoholic who's been going along fine for a while, then suddenly goes on a bender out of nowhere."

"Or a person who's been doing well setting aside time for Sabbath, then spends the whole day cleaning?"

He shrugs with a small smile.

Later I read the article for myself: "Just before you give up on a long-practiced routine, you freak out. It's a final desperate attempt by the oldest parts of your brain to keep getting rewarded . . . [The extinction burst is] a temporary increase in an old behavior, a plea from the recesses of your brain."[3]

"This is fascinating," I say to myself. I consider the ways my identity is wrapped up in notions of being in control, competent, on top of everything all the time. Clearly I derived some satisfaction from being that person, and for almost six months now, I've attempted to be someone else, at least once a week. It's no wonder that the old "me" would rebel.

It would be nice if this were really the last gasp of that person. She's not all that much fun, I'm discovering. But I suspect we'll be seeing more of her before the year is done.

* * *

Since the shooting in Tucson back in January, I've been thinking about the role of technology on the Sabbath. If Sabbath is about *not* being indispensable—about resting in the fact that the world goes on without us—then shouldn't that impact our consumption of media and news? I know many folks go without television and Internet on Sabbath, although I have a friend, a Seventh-Day Adventist, who admits she reads Facebook on the Sabbath. It's her way of connecting with loved ones.

I've decided to extend Sabbath into my tech habits, too. If I'm not on the computer that much, then it should be easy to sign off for a day, right? I'm a little nervous though. What if I go through withdrawal? But it feels right to try.

So the next Friday I sign off on Facebook: "I'm taking the weekend off from the computer. See you Sunday."

I am not one who spends hours on the computer on weekends. But it was the cement that filled in the cracks. I'd check Facebook in the morning, or put off the postdinner dishes with a quick perusal of Google Reader. It was beginning to feel like a cigarette break.

I wonder to myself if the Facebook fast will become harder later—is another extinction burst in my future?—but for now, it feels fine.

The Work of Sabbath: Fast from One Thing

The tech Sabbath suggests yet another approach to Sabbath—to go about one's day as usual, even if that includes work or errands, but to fast from one thing. Too tethered to your iPhone? Thoughts coming in 140-character bursts due to Twitter overload? Perhaps Sabbath can be nothing more than unplugging one's devices and focusing on the here and now.

Or are you a supercommuter? Do whatever you want on your Sabbath, as long as you don't get in the car. Fast from driving.

Fitness fanatic? Let the Sabbath be the day you let your body rest. Fast from exercise.

The Sabbath may also be a day to fast from abstract things, like worry or snarkiness. (I have a pastor friend who began a sermon in Lent by saying, "I once tried to give up sarcasm for Lent. *That* went well.") It's easier said than done, but giving something up for one day a week feels more manageable than seven.

I even wonder about Sabbath as a day to fast from a diet. Disclaimer: I'm not a doctor. There's a whole host of medical reasons why some people should not break their diets. But for folks who are simply trying to have a healthier lifestyle, it's possible that a day to "feast" may help set Sabbath apart. Feasting is certainly part of the Jewish Shabbat–good food and wine are an integral part of the day. If you're on a diet, Sabbath can be a fast from the fast.

Recently I have been so busy with church stuff that I've felt like every available moment has been filled with work. It's all thinking stuff, and I realize that I am completely spent mentally. (The recent extinction burst proves this.) So I take Friday as an extra sabbath day, but my Sabbath will be a fast from anything intellectual. I do several loads of laundry, which I normally avoid on Sabbath. Based on the traditional definitions of Sabbath, I've broken all the rules. I've changed my environment; I've tamed the chaos; I've worked. But it's not *intellectual* work. And with this different approach, an activity I normally find every excuse to avoid is strangely . . . restful.

*   *   *

Near the end of February, we are eating a late breakfast when we hear a familiar chirp that seems to come from right outside the kitchen window.

I stop midbite and look at Robert.

"Yep," he says bluntly. "I heard them the other day."

The birds are back.

Every year they take up residence in the exhaust vent of our range hood. We have a screen over the outside opening, yet they still get in somehow, build a nest, and lay eggs. We hear them when the weather is still cool enough that we aren't spending much time outside. Later in the spring, we begin to see them as well, when we sit on our deck on nice days. A streak of brown will catch my eye and I will see Mama Bird flutter her way to the duct and somehow wriggle inside, bits of straw and twig poking out of the hole.

Once we hear the noise, it's too late. We know that there's a nest, and soon, eggs on the nest, and we can't bear to close up the opening, to install a finer mesh and displace this little family. So we keep listening throughout the spring and early summer, as the chorus of chirps grows louder with increased numbers. And Robert and I lament that we didn't seal the opening last fall when the vent was uninhabited, and we bicker about whose fault it is.

"You were going to call someone."

"Yeah, but you never gave me recommendations of people to call."

I realize that there's no such thing as being caught up. That's an illusion. You vacuum the carpets, and the kitty pukes a hairball. You pay the bills and new ones arrive. You get every stitch of clothing washed, but there are still the clothes you're wearing—unless you're hoisting laundry baskets in your birthday suit, and even *I'm* not that obsessive.

The parade of tasks plods on, world without end. I get that.

But it seems sometimes that there are a million unfinished projects, worthwhile things, taunting us at every turn. There are consequences, however small, to having birds residing in our ductwork. The vent fan over the stove doesn't work properly. Maybe the motor will conk out eventually and need to be replaced. Our smoke alarm goes off when we burn something on the stove.

The birds aren't a big deal. But they're a reminder of one more thing we've failed to stay on top of. They're a living, chirping reminder that we have more to do than we have time to do it. Especially during this year of Sabbath.

"Look at the birds of the air . . ." I mutter to myself.

"What's that?" Margaret asks.

"It's a line from the Bible," I say. "Jesus tells people not to worry about their life, because if God cares about these sweet little creatures, God also cares about us" (Mt. 6:25–34).

I look at Robert, who's looking back at me with an *I get it. Do you get it?* expression.

I do.

8

March

It's not so much how busy you are, but why you are busy. The bee is praised. The mosquito is swatted.

—Mary O'Connor[1]

We've reached the halfway point. How has Sabbath changed me? How has it changed our family?

I can't answer the question fully without thinking about my red-handled scissors.

I got them in seventh grade for a home economics class. They're sewing scissors, which I used to cut out material for a simple elastic-waist skirt (blue plaid) and throw pillows for my sister that spelled out her name: K-A-T-I-E. But I don't sew anymore, so these scissors now live in our kitchen junk drawer. They're used for paper, clothing tags, clamshell packaging, and even the occasional stray wisp of hair. They're left-handed scissors, so as a lefty, they're precious to me. They're as tight and sharp as they were when I was twelve.

They're gone now.

One Friday in early March, my kids and I have a flurry of a day, getting errands done before Saturday's Sabbath. We grocery shop, we shoe shop, and we take cardboard to the recycling center. Margaret and James hand me boxes to load in the car, fighting over whose turn it is, while I slash through old packing tape to make everything flat and compact.

As I slam the back hatch, I turn to Margaret, hand her the scissors, and say, "Please put these back in the junk drawer for me."

She does not do that.

I discover they are gone because the weather stripping is coming off the bottom of our front door and I want to snip off that flapping tail so it won't flop around every time we open or close the door. The realization of the missing scissors leads to a brief but fruitless search and a short interrogation of Margaret, who has no idea where she's put them, bless her heart. I suspect that she absentmindedly dropped them into the trash can that's right next to the junk drawer—a likely occurrence since she did the same thing with a spoon at dinner the previous week.

I discover they are gone on Saturday, our sabbath day. That's the day we *don't* cut loose weather stripping from the front door . . . except that we do. I do. And I am reminded that they are gone at least twice more on that supposed day of rest. A new box of cat litter sits in the hallway—*ooh, the cat boxes could use a top-off.* A stubborn plastic tag on the previous day's clothing purchase from Target—*would really like to wear that today.* But no scissors.

I am mystified that, six full months into the Sabbath experiment, I still fight the impulse to work around the house. "Amazing," I tell Robert. "It isn't my commitment to Sabbath that stops me from doing this stuff. It's the lack of proper tools." The work still calls to me on the Sabbath. Even after half a year.

It's complicated. The fact that we anticipate the arrival of each Saturday with the giddy relief of kids at Christmas suggests that there's something right about it. But the impulse to tidy, to beautify, to make everything all better is always there.

And that's what this year has been about: a commitment to something simple but not easy. A resolution to stop changing things. To stop controlling the chaos for one blasted, blessed day.

The whereabouts of the scissors remain a mystery that may never be solved. The greater mystery, perhaps, is what is happening within me that resists stopping each week, that bristles against the simple, gracious invitation to let things be.

*   *   *

Even as I find myself nagged by work on the Sabbath, something else is happening that pulls me in the opposite direction.

When we started this experiment, I did so thinking it would give me the energy I needed for the rest of my life. I thought of the Sabbath in utilitarian terms: the day of rest would recharge my batteries and help me get even more done. I also thought the quality of my work would improve—a great benefit!

I have read the studies demonstrating the need for down time. Creativity thrives on fallow times—times of daydreaming, puttering, and playing. I interpreted these studies to mean that, because I rested every seventh day, my creative output would be even greater on the other six.

But in fact the opposite is happening. Sabbath is making me want to do even less the rest of the time. I'm starting to revise my life, declining opportunities that I might have jumped at previously. An editor asks me to help out on a project I've participated in many times before, and I say, "No, thanks." Faced each evening with the option to blast through more of the to-do list or to let some things go, I am more comfortable letting go. (I tell Robert I've declined some things and he says, "Really? So you could be even busier than you are now?" OK, maybe I'm the only one noticing an incremental difference.)

I have clergy friends who go weeks between days off. Others take Sabbath time as they can, but a weekly sacred time seems unthinkable. Some of this is happenstance—a surge of pastoral needs in their churches, fewer staff to share the work—but some of it is temperament. As many of my clergy colleagues take larger churches and more prestigious positions, I feel content with the pace of my little country church in the middle of the city. We have our busy times, and as we grow, we are deepening our ministry and getting more active in the community. But I do not miss the night meetings at the larger church I used to serve. Long days are frequent in many large and/or understaffed churches—and, incidentally, are all too common for other kinds of workers, too. With unemployment as high as it is, the people who do have jobs find themselves taking on the workload of former coworkers who've been laid off. They have little leverage to complain; they're "lucky to have this job."

I wish for everyone to have a satisfying job and a living wage. At the same time, I wonder whether the current economic crisis in our country is a wake-up call. Infinite growth and consumption is the trajectory we've been on as a culture, and it's unsustainable. Is there a simpler, more viable way to live? Does Sabbath provide a small portal through which we glimpse a better world?

Meister Eckhart, a Christian mystic and philosopher from the fourteenth century, said that the spiritual life is a process of subtraction.[2] Similarly, Henri Nouwen characterized the Christian life as a steady progression of downward mobility.³ Humility and simplicity are the signs of a life in Christ. As I begin to say "no" more often, I wonder if Sabbath might be winnowing my life into something more vital.

*   *   *

During March, some beloved family friends come for a visit with their daughter, who is between Caroline and Margaret's age. Sunday after church is Sabbath time, and we all decide to go to the zoo. Along with our houseguests and their seven-year-old daughter, we meet up with other friends of theirs, a young couple with a toddler. With so many children, it's a lot of shuffling around: waiting for one another at various turns and hanging back while kids watch the sea otters jump in and out of the water—a lot longer than we adults care to watch, but the children's laughs are addictive.

Margaret begins to get thirsty, and all the nearby water fountains are bone dry. I try to distract her by telling her that we'll be on the lookout for one as we walk, and look at that cute prairie dog! Nothing works.

I decide to leave the group and take her to find a water fountain, however far away it might be. "Margaret, we are going to find a water fountain!" I assure her. We walk about a third of the length of the zoo before we find a functioning one, an old model that burbles enthusiastically all over her shirt.

Then she is miserable because her shirt is wet—it's sunny but still chilly in early March. And just like that, she's done. She's tired of walking, tired of being at the zoo. She's ready to go.

We've got enough cars that she and I can leave. But we are as far from a car as we could possibly be. So I decide to give her a choice: "If you want to leave right now, we can leave right now. Nobody else is ready to leave, so you will need to walk with me to the smaller car, which is parked about thirty minutes away. Or, we can stay with the group, leave when they leave, and have Daddy pick us up at the exit in the van." She nods gravely, taking it all in.

"So which do you choose?" I ask. "More walking and leave now, or less walking and leave later?"

"I want to leave with you right now."

"You realize that you're going to walk farther this way and be more tired than if we stayed with the group?"

"Yes. I want to leave with you right now."

OK then.

My rule when I'm out with my children is that I cannot, or rather *will* not, carry them when they're tired of walking. They're too old for that and so is my back. My concession to them is that whenever they need to stop along the way, I will stop–however often that is.

I've wondered if this is a decent compromise or overly indulgent of me. A friend of mine with college-age daughters bristles when I tell her my taking-breaks method. "I get what you're trying to do," she said, "And even though I get it, my Calvinist background is really resisting that. In the world I grew up in, you do not cater to children."

Right or wrong, going at a child's pace is hard work all its own. It's tough to keep breathing normally and not get snappish when they request a break, having taken one only sixty seconds before. I sense that they do it to test me, to see whether I'm really serious about letting them take as long as they want.

Margaret exploits this practice with particular relish. At one point we are stopping every fifty feet or so. We stop so she can try out the bench or perch on a handrail for a while. We slow down so she can walk on the curb, balance-beam style. We stop for a photo on the big ZOO sign at the entrance. We stop to make friends with a little dog in the neighborhood.

I wish I could say it is enjoyable, but it is frequently excruciating. *Let's just get there!* I yell in my head. But as promised, we stop every time she wants. And wonder of wonders, she suddenly doesn't seem so tired anymore, and she's forgotten about her wet shirt.

She wasn't tired in the sense of physical fatigue. She was tired of having to conform to an entire group's pace, interest, and schedule. It is so rare that she gets to be completely in charge of our agenda. We either pander to the lowest common denominator (her little brother), which often means leaving before she's ready, or we go at her big sister's speed, making allowances for James but expecting Margaret to keep up. The trials of the middle child.

That weekend, the walk from the zoo to the car is my most significant Sabbath moment. It isn't easy, and it doesn't always feel good. Like many Sabbath times I've had this year, it is beneficial and uncomfortably itchy at the same time. But there is a certain wonder in glimpsing Margaret's pace without outside forces intervening. I feel I know my child more deeply now.

The Work of Sabbath: Saying Yes

"No" gets a bad rap, but I'm a fan. It is a gracious word because it conveys limits, which we all need. Many times, no is necessary in order to protect a bigger yes. I've been saying no more to outside requests and expectations on me lately.

An average day of parenting also involves a generous helping of no:

"No, you cannot play outside until you've finished your homework."
"No, we do not have time to ride bikes right now . . . kitty needs to go to the vet."
"No, we will not have ice cream for dinner."

But too often with my children, it's my own laziness that forms the word no. I say no because the result will be messy, inconvenient, or loud. No is a way of protecting boundaries, but it's also a way of seizing control, asserting one's authority, or closing oneself off to what could be an exciting, unpredictable adventure.

Along with our parental no-saying, there are the reminders of manners, the urges not to hit, and the prompts to use kind words. Robert and I don't needle our children with corrections, but it's our job to help them learn how to be in the world. I start to wonder whether Sabbath might be a time to ease up. I take seriously my role as a parent, to help my children become the people they're meant to be. But maybe that job goes beyond molding their young minds; maybe it means living with them in a space in which we are all being molded. A Sabbath space.

I explain this to Robert and ask what he thinks: "I have a weird idea. What if on Sabbath we tried to say yes to our kids? Within reason, of course."

He makes a face. "I don't know . . . don't kids need consistency? Will that be too confusing?"

"I'm not saying we let them pummel each other. But I'd like to see what happens if we ease up on that day. In parenting you have to pick your battles. I'm saying that maybe on the Sabbath we don't fight quite as many."

"OK, let's try it, but I don't think we should tell them that we're doing it. That could be a disaster. Let's just do it and see what happens."

One of the rules of improvisational theater is to "yes-and." When people are building a scene, there's a basic agreement that the players will not contradict the idea offered by the others. They will accept what has been said and build on it. It's a generous way to be in the world but hard to sustain all the time.

"Yes, I will play Thomas trains with you." (Again and again and again.)

"Yes, you can wear that princess costume to the park." (Even though it's thirty-five degrees outside. I'll bring a coat along.)

"Yes, we can eat lunch on the back porch." (Even though that means more effort and we're tired.)

The experience is simultaneously tiring and gratifying. At first, I feel a bit like a waitress, until I recall that I don't need to get Caroline a drink; she can do that kind of thing herself. But the kids' joy at being heard and responded to is contagious, and rather than take advantage of our agreeableness, they are more agreeable in return.

We've arrived at yet another dimension of Sabbath: Once a week, we can "yes-and" our children. Rather than be confused by the seeming lack of consistency, they get that Sabbath is a different kind of day with different rules and rhythms. Saying yes on Sabbath means that they accept our no's on other days more easily. Sabbath also becomes a laboratory for the rest of the week, as we realize that we could probably say yes more than we do.

The biblical story is a story of "yes-and." Countless ordinary people say yes to unexpected and sometimes off-the-wall requests:

Build an ark, Noah.

Tell Pharaoh to let my people go, Moses.

Go preach to Nineveh, Jonah.

Buy this field even though the people are in exile, Jeremiah.

Speak to this pile of dry bones so they can live, Ezekiel.

Have a baby out of wedlock, Mary.

Feed my lambs, Peter.

These are all big yeses. Vigorous yeses. Life-changing yeses. I have enough trouble saying yes to one more game of Fairy-opoly. But maybe yes is habit-forming. Maybe when I'm called upon to do something big, all these small yeses will make it easier. Perhaps by forming the word with our lips, we learn to form it with our lives.

*   *   *

"Let's make Hogwarts and Hogsmeade!" Margaret shouts as she dumps the bin of blocks onto the floor.

That's an easy yes. The kids are learning to entertain themselves so well that they don't need me to get involved with their games as much, but it's been too long since I've really immersed myself in playing with them. My kids are endlessly fascinating, and watching them play is one of my favorite pastimes . . . but many games for young children aren't all that interesting. Chutes and Ladders, Candy Land . . . these are good excuses to be with your kids but in terms of sheer entertainment they leave something to be desired. Even a child's imaginative play has a lot of repetition and bossy imperatives:

"Put this on."

"Now you say this."

"Let's play hide and seek: you hide behind the curtain. Again."

But today's Harry Potter–inspired construction project is truly collaborative. Hogwarts castle comes together complete with arches and turrets, fashioned with plain wooden blocks. We prompt each other with reminders of different elements of the landscape: Hagrid's hut, the Three Broomsticks, and shouldn't we use these colorful blocks for Honeydukes candy shop? One of James's cars becomes the Weasley's flying car, caught in the Whomping Willow tree.

For the Quiddich field, we pilfer from a board game to find long thin trays that become bleachers. Caroline later joins in with a handmade broomstick, made from a bamboo skewer wrapped on one end with construction paper she has cut into fringe. They tie it to a piece of string and fly it around the field.

Their play stretches out over the remainder of the day.

We have a soundtrack while we build and play: Robert is picking out a sonata on the piano. The sound of an adult in our house playing the piano is a true Sabbath sound. We are both pretty rusty. There is no utility, no useful purpose for our piano playing other than pure enjoyment. It is a joyful noise to the Lord and each other–a joyful, halting, stumbling-note Sabbath noise.

* * *

For the first time since the Sabbath year began, a Sabbath has been interrupted because of an urgent ministry issue. As pastor of a small congregation, there are a lot fewer emergencies, but they happen. *Six months is a pretty good streak,* I think as I read the text message.

In this case, it's not a life-or-death situation, but it's something that tugs on me mentally. It seems like an emergency to the person involved, but it could have waited until the next day. I do the minimum needed to dispatch the issue, but it continues to grate. How will I keep it from hanging over me the rest of the day? Intellectually I know that I am not indispensable. This can wait. I can let time work on it. But emotionally, it still lodges in my consciousness.

I try a mental trick I picked up somewhere, a wordless prayer that I use after preaching sometimes. Often following a sermon I think about things I wish I'd said, or I hold on to a critical comment someone has made, and it's hard to move on. When this happens, I imagine that the sermon is a kite I am flying. I feel the string, heavy and urgent in my hand as I let out more and more line. The kite flies higher and higher until I can barely see it. The tail whips around beneath it, occasionally catching the sunlight.

When I'm almost out of line–when the kite's almost out of sight–I cut the string. I feel the relief of not holding onto the kite anymore and watch the wind carry it away as the empty line flutters to the ground. I don't know where it's going but it doesn't matter; it's not mine anymore.

Thankfully, the prayer works, and I can let the emotional energy around the church issue float away. I trust that the kite will find its way down to me again when it's time. Because this is ministry, it could just as easily bean me on the side of the head. But I can handle that too, when it happens.

Sabbath Hack: Cheat Once

The e-mail arrives, asking kids to sign up to sell Girl Scout cookies in front of the neighborhood grocery store. February and March are Girl Scout cookie time. Caroline didn't sell many cookies on her own–it fell through the cracks, like so many other things–but she sold enough to win the bandana. It's become a family joke: every year she aspires for the T-shirt, and every year she ends up with the bandana. (How do other kids manage to sell a hundred or more boxes while still keeping up with soccer practice, hip-hop class, and Mandarin?)

But booth sales we can do. It's a fun chance for the girls to cut up with one another in between being cute in that ultrapolite way with bemused customers clutching reusable bags. I check the dates, choose two of the four, and respond, "Yes! We're in." I wish all e-mail queries were so easy to solve.

One problem: the dates are on Saturday, the Sabbath. Oh, yeah. How easily I forget.

I decide to try a new Sabbath hack: I decide to cheat. I decide we can carve out one to two hours for this very specific activity and still take the time before and after as Sabbath. It's a much better option than blowing off the troop on the one hand, or blowing off Sabbath on the other.

I think about Jesus, who healed on the sabbath day to the dismay of many folks around him. I wonder if he returned to Sabbath observance afterward. I like to think that he stepped in and out of Shabbat as needed. Maybe the pace of Sabbath allowed him to see clearly the people who needed him most. And perhaps these encounters gave a new shape and character to the rest of his sabbath day rather than being an inconvenient detour. I remember the good Samaritan experiment at Princeton Seminary, in which people's willingness to help another person was directly related to their lack of hurry.

Partly because it's bracketed by Sabbath, I see the booth sale as veiled in loveliness and not at all a chore. I watch the girls stack boxes of Thin Mints and Tagalongs with great precision. I marvel at one girl's ability to make change so rapidly. I get a chance to see Caroline's silly side, which her friends bring out in her. When we get home, we feel oddly refreshed for the remainder of the day. Ready for rest.

Choosing only one bit of work for Sabbath requires discernment. It becomes a mental game, to find the one most important thing that must be done and to put parentheses around it in order to protect the rest of the day.

There are times that an entire day of rest is not feasible, thanks to scheduling or other factors. And I know that some would view this practice as a wholesale rejection of Sabbath. So be it. As for me, I'll take a messy and real imperfection over an impossible perfection any day.

* * *

A few years ago, I was in a retreat in which the leader described a group of desert monks who wove baskets every day to earn alms for the poor. If the baskets went unsold, they took them apart and remade them. It was a means of holiness, a way of loving God, the leader said, to make the same basket again and again.

"How lovely," the person next to me murmured. I rolled my eyes. Why don't they keep the first basket, try to sell it again, and find something else useful to do?

At another time in my life, I might have seen the remaking of baskets as a charming expression of spiritual simplicity. Now I am much more pragmatic about such things. As a pastor/parent, people are counting on me for concrete, practical things: A fresh sermon on Sunday morning. Food in the lunch box every weekday. Clean clothing in the chest of drawers. An insightful article. New mittens in the winter to replace the worn-out ones. Five dollars attached to the permission slip. Cans of cat food stacked atop the fridge. I barely have time to do the important things *once*; the idea of making the same basket, year after year, seems self-indulgent, not endearing.

Then again, love involves constant unweaving. Our lives are a braiding and rebraiding of baskets. I lead the church I serve through holy days and seasons, year after year, again and again: Advent, Christmas, Lent, Easter. Each year is different and yet the same. Robert and I have had variations on the same argument about household chores for sixteen years. I'm not sure how much progress we make, but it's important to renegotiate all the time. It's bedtime and James wants his Lightning McQueen book again: the one I don't need to read anymore because I have it memorized.

Paul wrote, "Love is patient; love is kind; love is not envious or boastful . . . love never ends" (1 Cor. 13:4, 8). I would add, "Love is repetitive; love is inefficient. Love is not a 'productive' use of time. It does not produce many lasting artifacts. The work of love never ends."

I'm listening to an interview with Jean Varnier, who founded the L'Arche community, where people with mental disabilities live in dignity and tenderness with one another. He says that a business-man came to him, impressed with his work, and said, "Give me the formula and I'll open 300 L'Arches within two years." (I'm guessing that businessman would also roll his eyes at the desert fathers and their rebraided baskets.)

But Varnier shook his head, because it doesn't work like that. His interviewer quotes him as saying that L'Arche is not a solution, but a sign.[4]

Ahh . . . love is a sign. Sabbath is a sign.

I still recoil from the "uselessness" of rebraiding the same basket year after year. But yes: my life is not a thing to solve. It is a sign—of the holiness in small things and the timelessness in the moment.

9

April

It would be good for the world to have to observe the Sabbath, a day of rest where everyone tries not to exert their force on the world, and is grateful to God, and tries not to squash any life, not even bugs, and all the malls and fast-food restaurants and TVs are shut down. It seems like the world would be about a thirty-thousand-times better place.

—Debbie Blue[1]

With the coming of spring, Sabbath takes on a different flavor. Instead of hunkering down, we're throwing open the windows. The front door slams incessantly with kids scurrying in and out. Baking bread doesn't have the cozy appeal it did when the temperature barely hovered above freezing. Robert has bottled his final batch of beer for a while—the basement will soon be too warm for fermentation to occur.

Music has always been an important element of Sabbath—it's part of how we mark the time and set it aside—but the soundtrack has changed. During the winter we listened to a lot of acoustic guitar and piano. Now the music is energetic, world beat stuff. We are coming to life.

We eat our Sabbath meals outside on the back deck. (The lunch-time Bagel Bites continue to be a winner! Easy and popular.) The kids bounce in their chairs, and I try not to be bothered by the bare flower pots with their crusted-over soil and brown leggy stalks. I really should take some time to plant, but I don't.

The children take an interest in the hose and sprinkler, and I say yes to their eagerness, wondering how chilly it will be in the April breeze. They run back and forth, leaping over thin streams of water until their lips turn blue. They towel off, warm up, and ride their bikes and scooters down the street. They spend hours going around and around, making up obstacle courses for each other: "Ride to the mailbox and back, then ring your bell twice, then go around once while singing 'Old McDonald.'"

We visit a new playground, where James pushes an empty swing, catches it by one chain on the return, and laughs when it wobbles in his hand. "Isn't that funny, Mommy?" I don't normally find the laws of physics amusing, but his guffaws win me over. Margaret runs toward a cluster of trees to see if there's a creek nearby. The land slopes downward, and it looks like there should be water there. The Bradford pear tree snows on her as she goes. She returns disappointed but not empty handed: no creek but two perfect white blossoms, plucked just for me from the dusting on the ground.

We walk the neighborhood, detectives in search of daffodils, sleuthing for any sign of spring. Ours bloom later than many of our neighbors. I'm insecure enough about our yard skills that I think we must be doing something wrong. Our azaleas will inexplicably bloom in the fall some years. But then I decide it's OK. Sabbath means our sense of time is out of sync with other families around us; maybe the yard is following our lead.

Sabbath in April means pulling chairs out to the front porch during a sudden rainstorm, watching the water tumbling over itself as it cascades down the street.

Sabbath in April means blowing bubbles on the front porch and watching how long they last now that the air has more humidity. I watch them drift, and remember that one of Caroline's favorite words when she was learning to talk was "bubble." She would use it to describe anything that pleased her. Cat rubbing up against her leg? *Bubble.* A taste of ice cream? *Bubble!* I watch the children chasing the fragile iridescent globes around our front stoop, and I agree, little ones. *Bubble.* Really, no other word will do.

*　*　*

April is the month that our neighborhood comes to life with home improvement and spring cleaning projects. The local Boy Scout troop takes orders for mulch, which they deliver in large bags and stack on people's driveways. We see an increase in trucks on our street: landscaping, painting, AC repair. Storage pods appear as people clean out garages and attics.

We are not immune to the spring cleaning bug. This month Robert is gassing up the lawn mower and power-washing the deck. I am clearing winter cobwebs out of doorways and dusting miniblinds. Spring is the time for washing the comforters and rotating the winter and summer clothes in the closets. Like animals that have awakened from a winter hibernation, we feel industrious. We dream about home improvement projects.

But our time for these pursuits is limited by this year's Sabbath focus. There are several big projects that we've been putting off, in some cases for years: repainting the upstairs, an update to the kitchen, a basement reorganization. But this year, it's the little projects that are collecting dust, too. A kitchen drawer broke several months ago, and its contents are sitting in a soup tureen in the corner of another room. Caroline got a poster at Christmas that we've managed to frame, but it's still sitting on the floor, propped against the wall rather than hanging on it. And have those curtains *ever* been taken down and washed?

There are dozens more projects where those came from. None of them requires all that much time or energy, but when one entire day each weekend is already spoken for, things start to pile up.

A friend of mine and an admirer of our Sabbath experiment says, "Here's something I struggle with: doing work on the weekend that isn't exactly fun but would help us have fun later. For example, shopping for new patio furniture. It's not Sabbath by any stretch, but it would contribute to a nicer experience in our backyard in the long run. How do you handle that?"

How, indeed?

"I don't know," I say to Robert as we look at the disheveled state of our house. "Maybe we need to chuck Sabbath for three or four weeks and blast through some of this stuff." We talk about it for a while but don't come to a decision. The next weekend, we pursue Sabbath as usual.

"So much for the home projects," Robert says at the end of the day, not unhappily.

"What a switch!" I say. "Remember in Iona when we first decided to do Sabbath? It took us forever to actually *do* it. Everything else got in the way. Now it's *Sabbath* that's become the habit we can't give up."

Here is where friends with grown children inevitably tell me that nobody reaches their deathbed, or even the empty nest, wishing they'd spent more time cleaning or doing home improvement. Relationships trump everything. I get it. And people have different levels of tolerance for chaos and clutter. But I'm not willing to dismiss the importance of a home that's tidy and in decent repair either.

One of the deceptions I hear sometimes, especially among some church folks, is this idea that the physical stuff of our lives doesn't really matter because we are focused on loftier, spiritual matters. I believe this is dead wrong. It certainly doesn't reflect the story of a God who became a human being, who took on flesh and bone and blood. Jesus cared about physical stuff; he was *made* of physical stuff. He attended a wedding and turned water into wine—good wine, too, not the cheap stuff in the box. His teachings dealt with money, possessions, the harvest, the vineyard. The life of Jesus wasn't focused on esoteric matters of spirit. It was grounded in this real, physical world—a world that, for me, consists of sermons, bills, and dishes.

The basement needs a thorough cleaning. But we're married to Sabbath at least through the summer, so it's not likely to happen. We need to be OK with that.

Sabbath Hack: Borrow from the *Looney Tunes*

Remember those old *Looney Tunes* cartoons in which a hungry character looks at its prey and sees a juicy steak where the head is supposed to be? Or when the guy who's down on his luck finds a singing frog and begins to see dollar signs?

I've started doing the same thing with the clutter and piled-up projects in our house. Rather than looking at an unfinished task and seeing what we've failed to do, I picture what that unfinished task represents: namely, something important that we *have* done.

So when I look at our cluttered garage full of broken rakes and household items we've discarded but haven't yet gotten rid of—some of which have been with us for years—I try not to see our failure in getting the garage cleaned out. Instead I see all those times we pedaled bikes up and down our street, gasping to reach the top of the steep hill, then soaring down to the bottom again.

Every time I open the cabinet under the sink, I see a mess of bottles, desiccated sponges, and aluminum foil. For nine years they have begged for an intervention from the Container Store. I try to see something else instead: I see Caroline hunched over a ball of yarn and a chaos of stitches as I teach her, slowly, to knit. With this new vision, the undone thing isn't a sign of neglect or failure. It's a testimony that something else is more important at this moment of our lives.

Even if you don't observe Sabbath, a shift in perception is helpful. It doesn't ever all get done. We need to train our vision. We see failure when we should see alternatives. Better to focus on the good and important things we did do instead of berating ourselves for falling short of an ideal.

Robert's grandmother remembers a time when her children were young and a fussy neighbor wrinkled his nose at the bare patches of grass in her yard. "You really ought to do something about that," he said with disdain. She responded, "I'll grow grass when I stop growing children."

I applauded when I heard that story.

*   *   *

The worst of the spring colds is finally fading into lingering sniffles and the occasional cough that echoes through the house at night. It has been an exhausting few weeks, juggling work and multitasking with sick kids. "How come you guys wait until the previous kid is completely better before getting sick yourself?" I chide when a new fever emerges. Winter and early spring are one long circus train of illnesses.

Church has been busy too, with congregational meetings, church officer training, and retreats. I'm so tired that I don't even have the mental energy to describe how tired I am, how in need of Sabbath I am. But I don't need to. I don't need to justify taking a day off; I don't need to prove to anyone that I've earned it; I don't need to advocate for myself. The calendar is my advocate. If it's Saturday, it's sabbath day. We will all stop together. *Thank God.*

It's Saturday morning, and I am beginning to stretch out into a day of Sabbath—we're planning to see the cherry blossoms downtown, an experience of joyful beauty particular to the DC region. Suddenly Robert says, "I was thinking . . . do you think we should have Sabbath tomorrow instead of today? It's supposed to rain this afternoon, but tomorrow's gonna be gorgeous, much better for cherry blossoms. We can run errands and stuff today."

"Oh my God, no no no!" I blurt out. Tears spring to my eyes.

Robert looks at me, surprised. I am too: *Wow, what's that about?*

It's the calculating that gets me, the endless decisions about what to do and when. This is our life. The lawn needs mowing; well, when's it supposed to rain? How long will these errands take? How long do we have until the little ones have their prenap meltdown?

My work life is full of these calculations. I have an hour between the clergy luncheon and coffee with a parishioner. Should that be sermon time or catching up on phone calls? The kids are napping. Should I plow through my backlog of reading material or write that newsletter article?

The fancy church word for this calculation is *discernment*: deciding the right course of action for the moment, day, life. One of the best-known (and in my opinion, least understood) stories in the New Testament is Jesus' visit to the home of Martha and Mary, two sisters who host Jesus and his friends. Martha, cooking in the kitchen, is distracted and resentful. She's tired of doing all the work while Mary sits at Jesus' feet listening to his teaching. Jesus rebukes Martha, and the comment stings: Martha should focus on the one thing needful, like her sister Mary, who has chosen "the better part" (Lk. 10:38–42).

The story is not about the importance of education over household tasks. It's about mindfulness—that whatever we're doing is the right thing for that moment and that we're doing it wholeheartedly.

But for parents, and those who work, and especially amid the combination of the two, the one thing needful can change rapidly, requiring a new calculation minute by minute. That can be exhausting.

I explain all this to Robert, who's curious and concerned about my outburst. "I don't want to calculate Sabbath, too. Sabbath is Sabbath and we go with it. I'm exhausted. I don't care about the weather."

"Got it. OK, why don't you take the morning and rest. I'll take the kids out for a while we'll see how it goes. Today, tomorrow—whatever is fine."

I go back to bed and sleep until they come home. I wake up feeling better and ready to tackle some chores. The next day I'm eager for cherry blossoms, and he's right—it's a dazzling day.

We decide to bypass the huge crowds around the tidal basin and Jefferson Memorial and head to the grounds of the U.S. Capitol, which has a small but impressive collection of trees. We park a few blocks away, and as usual, Margaret insists on walking on every curb and short wall we see. Caroline is surly and doesn't want to be there. She gripes about having to walk. We are cheerful in spite of her grouchiness, which unfortunately seems to egg her on.

No sooner do we make it to the Capitol grounds than Margaret informs us she needs to go to the bathroom. Every public building we've passed is closed and locked. We make a detour to the botanical gardens, which is a few blocks from the Capitol, to look around and use the facilities.

Inside, Caroline is transformed: she becomes serene, peaceful. Later she says, "I learned something about myself today, Mommy: I learned that being around plants and green growing things makes me feel more relaxed and happy."

The Work of Sabbath: Authenticity

Caroline's comment about the green growing things suggests another understanding of Sabbath: a place to be authentic.

My mini-meltdown with Robert was an authentic moment in which I was able to articulate something I hadn't even voiced to myself: namely, my weariness with managing things, especially after several weeks of kid illnesses and work pileups. I didn't want to have an "ideal" Sabbath experience on the "ideal" day; I wanted to have whatever authentic Sabbath experience happened to come to me on the day we had set aside.

The Jewish Sabbath emphasizes bringing one's best self to God, which ideally includes tidying the house, showering, and even dressing up for the Friday night meal. I respect this intentionality in its own way. It's the same impulse that leads some people to dress up for church. It is a way of showing respect.

But maybe we also show respect for the Holy in our lives when we bring our real selves, not our clean and made-up ones. One of my favorite names for God comes from Barbara Brown Taylor: the "Really Real."[2] Jesus shows us what that name means—he was uniquely and completely himself, free of guile or artifice. On the Sabbath, I seek to be really real before the One who is the genuine article.

As a preacher, I realized early on in the Sabbath experiment that I would need to finish my sermons prior to Saturday in order to fully engage in Sabbath—no more "Saturday night specials" (though ending Sabbath right after the kids go to bed has given me a cushion, thankfully). For the most part, I've been able to finish the sermon on Thursday or Friday. Doing so is a time-management challenge, to be sure.

But the bigger challenge is internal: I have to be willing to accept the "good enough" sermon and to trust that preaching every single week requires ongoing steadfastness and commitment, not perfection or a constant striving for brilliance. I take great pride in what I write and deliver to the congregation I serve. But I've also learned that a less-than-perfect offering can soar in the hearts of one's listeners when that offering is soaked in the kind of authenticity that Sabbath fosters. In other words, I've sacrificed some time and technical artistry in order to make room for Sabbath, but Sabbath has enriched my preaching in return.

On a mundane level, I consider it a successful Sabbath if I don't have to wear makeup all day. Maybe we've all gone too far toward respectability, which can hide our true selves—our dysfunctional, cranky selves. Maybe it's time for a little authenticity instead.

Our family doesn't have it all together. We're tired and grumpy a lot of the time on Sabbath. Sometimes we manage to give ourselves permission to be not at our best.

Other times, we seem *more* authentically ourselves on that day. I, for one, breathe more deeply and laugh more easily than I do on other days.

In one of the gospels, Jesus tells a story about a party in which the host invites all the "right" people, the respectable people, and nobody shows up. So instead the host sends his servants into the streets to round up the "poor, the crippled, the blind, and the lame" to come and partake of the banquet that the upper crust couldn't be bothered to enjoy (Lk. 14:15–24).

In the same way, I feel myself welcomed to the Sabbath feast. I don't have to be "on." It's my prickly places, or my broken places, that need some time at the banquet.

*   *   *

With more than half of this experiment behind us, I'm starting to think about the future. What will the kids remember of this experience? I think back to my own childhood. What do I remember about the passage of time and how we spent our days?

I grew up in the 1970s and 1980s in a sleepy, friendly neighborhood in Houston, Texas. It was a small town in the middle of the nation's fourth largest city—we walked to school, took ballet at the recreation center, and spent all day every day at the pool during the summer. This idyllic childhood tipped over into a latchkey adolescence when my parents divorced while I was in junior high. Life was full on either side of that cataclysm, but with different things.

Predivorce, we had church, softball, scouts, and slumber parties. Postdivorce, it was mom's job, babysitting my younger siblings, and the busyness of high school extracurriculars.

But through it all, I cannot remember a time when my mother or father hurried me. If I was late to things, I don't remember. If I was shooed along or rushed from place to place, I have no recollection of it. Yet surely our life was busy and full. There were four of us kids, after all, each with our own panoply of activities, not to mention haircuts, orthodontists, and trips to buy new shoes.

Was I up late in elementary school finishing my homework because the softball game had gone long? Was I asked to cut the book-reading short when it was time to go to piano, as my kids are? Have I blocked out these moments?

I wonder whether I don't remember being rushed and hurried because that's not the kind of thing that kids remember. I realize how much of this experiment has been a version of working parent insurance: for at least one day a week, I am not trying to stuff my children into the car to get somewhere. We're building memories as we model an alternative way of being. But whenever I blow my top with the kids, I think, *This is the mommy they'll remember, not the Sabbath one who agreed to play eight rounds of Don't Break the Ice.*

On the bulletin board in my study is a picture I cut from a magazine of a young girl drawing a picture. She is so serene, so absorbed in the task. Underneath I have written the words, "Today is their childhood." It's my reminder that today is all we have.

"Let the little children come to me," Jesus famously says (Mt. 19:14). Jesus represents a safe space, a grounded place of stability where little ones can come and be accepted. There is a set-apartness to Jesus' invitation. We have to take the time, make the effort. It's possible to have a transcendent moment in the thirty minutes between hip-hop class and T-ball, but something is lost in the sandwiching.

This afternoon, this Sabbath afternoon, the girls come home from playing across the street, and James and I are on the front porch. He has his bin of cars and trucks and is lining them up in his predictable rows. Then the girls come out with colored pencils and paper and begin to draw pictures for James, which we later tape to the wall in his room. "They drew my Mack truck and my blue truck and the school bus," he says. "Here, let me count them: one, two, three."

Today is their childhood.

*   *   *

"Sabbath time, huh?"

This is Robert talking. Last week I was feeling crispy-fried and overwhelmed, and now it's his turn. He's been slammed at work–too many meetings, not enough time to do the work created by the meetings. He's ready for some alone time. This is a challenge because so much of our Sabbath time is together. He feels guilty for needing some recreation time away from the kids . . . but he needs recreation time away from the kids.

A friend of mine recently asked me, "How do you do Sabbath when people's interests and needs are so different?" Her son loves riding horses, and the riding competitions are on Saturday. Meanwhile her daughter has other interests–there's no pleasing everyone. I recall her question as I look at Robert's stooped shoulders. He's game to go with the family flow, but sometimes the needs of the individual have to take precedence.

"I'll take the kids somewhere today," I reassure him. "Do what you need to do. Putter around the house, whatever."

I don't have a good answer to my friend's dilemma. Sabbath feels like a dance between the impulse for togetherness and the needs of the individual. Those boundaries are always being renegotiated. I have a friend who takes a Sabbath every Sunday, and when their children have sports commitments, the whole family goes along and cheers on their sibling. "That way at least we're 'together,'" she says. I know another family that observes a strict Sunday Sabbath. If there are sports with practices or games on Sunday, they don't do those sports.

The latter option has the advantage of being consistent, but there's no denying that a bit of the child's individuality is sacrificed to make it happen. Whether one takes a Saturday or a Sunday Sabbath, it's almost impossible to find a league that avoids the weekends altogether. Sports programs don't even respect Sunday morning–the traditional worship time for Christians–as off-limits. They certainly aren't going to avoid conflicting with something as fringe and countercultural as Sabbath. Difficult choices are inevitable, and each option comes with its own costs.

But today's choice is easy–give Robert some time for himself. I take the kids to the local dollar theater (that's way more than a dollar) to see a Disney movie. Naturally, the kids manage to disagree over this seemingly foolproof option; Margaret wails, "I don't want to do that!" What she *wants* to do isn't clear. I sigh. I'm tired of suggesting fun things, on Sabbath or otherwise, and having them go over like a trip to the dentist.

No offense to dentists.

She comes around, eventually, and we enjoy the movie. When we come home, Robert's smiling and his shoulders aren't so stooped.

* * *

Easter arrives. That morning, I marvel at the church I serve and what they have taught me about a different pace. Every Sunday following worship we have coffee and snacks so folks can chat. That's not an unusual practice in a church; what is unusual is the unhurried way that people connect with one another, like they have all the time in the world.

These folks are just as busy as any other group of people, and of course there's always someone who has to leave right after the service. But most people stay and visit for a spell. On Easter of all days, I expect hurry. I know that Easter dinners are waiting—plans with extended family, long drives to have a meal with friends on the other side of town. But coffee hour is sacred. It's a bit of communal Sabbath, every single Sunday. Even Easter.

My in-laws are here to spend the holiday with us. Easter can be hard for clergy; there are extra services the week leading up to it, and Easter services usually have a lot of moving parts: extra flowers, musicians, visitors. At the same time, the expectation of a fancy dinner is still out there—Easter is one of our feast days, after all, and for people who commemorate Lent with the giving up coffee or chocolate, there is a particular joy in breaking that fast.

But this year, Sabbath seems to be nudging us to let go of the big dinner and simplify. The weather is beautiful, so we have a picnic instead of a formal dinner. It's the right speed for our kids, and lots of items can be purchased or thrown together easily. We go to our favorite state park and nibble on cheese and crackers, pasta and vegetable salad, and fancy cookies while the kids dart from table to playground. Caroline helps catch James at the bottom of a long slide and Margaret is doing her unique dance without music.

New life abounds.

10

May

To allow oneself to be carried away by a multitude of conflicting concerns, to surrender to too many demands, to commit oneself to too many projects, to want to help everyone in everything, is to succumb to violence.

—Thomas Merton[1]

There once was a man, a humble man, who was called upon to be a leader among his people. Over time, the job description grew, as often happens with leaders. Not only did the people need to be led into some new challenges and opportunities, but they also needed to be cared for in the meantime. Their disputes needed mediation. Their questions needed answers.

This man, a good-hearted and attentive leader, saw no other option but to respond to the many requests that came his way. The work stretched out before him, day after day, with no end in sight. There was no relief for our hapless hero, who tended the throngs of needy people lined up before him as far as the eye could see.

One day, the man's father-in-law came to visit. He took one look at the situation and saw what the man, so immersed in nonstop need, could not see: the situation was unsustainable. Maybe it was the bags underneath our hero's eyes or the brittleness in his voice as he snapped at others. Or maybe it was the way the man slumped his shoulders, unable to find enjoyment in the things he used to love to do. Sooner or later, the man would collapse from exhaustion—and then what?

Finally, the elder man had seen enough. He pulled his son-in-law aside and said, "What you are doing is not good. You will surely wear yourself out." The younger man protested that the people needed him. He'd been specially chosen for this work.

The father-in-law offered him a new way: train other leaders who would be able to handle the minor things and take care of only the most important issues himself. He should save his energy for the most pressing matters, those tasks that were his to do and nobody else's.

What the more experienced man offered was an alternate vision, one in which the world did not depend on the efforts of one person. Other people could be trusted to do their part. The leader was not indispensable. He could ease up and the world would keep turning.

Some time later, that leader took a trip up a mountain. (Perhaps now he had time to do so because he was not working so much.) While he was there, he received an unprecedented gift and unparalleled responsibility: a set of stone tablets. The Ten Commandments.

One of these commandments had a special place in his heart. It was the fourth: to remember and keep holy the sabbath day, a day of rest. He understood this commandment in a way he wouldn't have before his father-in-law's intervention. Without that intervention, he would not have been able to receive God's commandment to rest and to see it as a joy—not a burden or an impossibility. He said a prayer of thanks for his father-in-law, Jethro.

The leader's name, of course, was Moses.

*   *   *

I adore this story, found in the eighteenth chapter of Exodus (with my embellishments), and don't understand why we don't hear it referenced more often. The situation is such a modern one. Biblical characters often seem too good to be true—or too dastardly—but here we see Moses as stressed-out middle manager. He doesn't have it all figured out. He's a bit of a workaholic. He doesn't know how to say no. My pastoral care professors in seminary would say he's "not very self-differentiated."

Jethro says, "What are you doing?" And Moses, perhaps a little defensively, says, "I am doing God's work. The people need me. This is important stuff."

Moses has fallen into what I've heard described as the Messiah Trap: a net that pulls people in because they believe two basic lies. One: if I don't do it, it won't get done. And two: everyone's needs take priority over mine.[2]

Jethro exposes the Messiah Trap as a lie: "What you are doing is not good." Remarkable. Moses *is* doing good. The work he does is important. And yet something about it is not good. Most of the over-worked, burned-out people I know have this same issue–they feel pulled by countless valuable, worthwhile pursuits: by lots of options to do good.

This story feels like it could have been written last week . . . except that we don't meet a lot of people named Jethro anymore. Which is a shame, because everybody needs a Jethro.

I have a few Jethros–people who help me remember that I'm not God, people who help me not to be consumed by good work. But my most effective Jethro is one who is no longer with us. My father died suddenly many years ago. His death occurred two days after I accepted my first call to ministry and two weeks before I became a parent.

Dad died of cardiac arrest. It was shocking, but if I'm completely honest, it was not truly surprising. He wasn't in good shape. He generally ate whatever he wanted. He didn't exercise regularly. He worked and traveled in a very stressful job. He stopped being a faithful blood donor when the Houston Blood Bank started putting the cholesterol count on the cards. "I don't want to know that!" he'd once joked to me.

Our bodies are complicated. We can't ever know all the physical, spiritual, and mental factors that affect a person's health. I can't say definitively that overwork and poor self-care killed my father. But his death speaks to me nevertheless, whenever I am tempted to wring all the productivity I possibly can out of my life: *What you are doing is not good.* Dad is my Jethro.

There was something powerful in the timing of his death, too, wedged in between two of the most important events of my life, a call to ministry and the beginning of parenthood. His death cautions me to be intentional in how I live my life. In the evenings, when I am faced with the decision of making one more phone call or getting on the treadmill, I think of him and put on my walking shoes. Or when I have an article to write and the kids want me to read them a story, I think of him and reach for *Knuffle Bunny.*

This whole Sabbath experiment, when I get down to it, is a reaction to the inevitability of death. I've often thought about Sabbath from the point of view of a parent–it's an attempt to savor the time we have with our children while they are small, to not be so distracted by the busyness of life that we forget to live. But I also experience Sabbath as a daughter whose father died way too soon. Our time is short on this earth. Rabbi Heschel expresses as much with devastating clarity: "Time to us is sarcasm, a slick treacherous monster with a jaw like a furnace incinerating every moment of our lives."[3]

I wish I'd had more time with Dad. I wish we'd spent more unhurried time together. So many of our conversations in those last years were on the run, between this and that. There was always more to say than we had time for. Sabbath doesn't solve this scarcity of time, of course. But it does give me hope that, by setting aside time for holiness to happen, it can and will. And I'll be awake enough to perceive it when it does. The Sabbath experiment probably owes more to my father than I ever realized.

His birthday is this month. He would have been sixty-four.

*   *   *

I am out of town the first week of May, meeting with a group of clergy I see every year called the Well. It's an intense few days. We write papers in advance of the meeting and spend each day reading and commenting on them. The week is also a lot of fun, a complete break from family responsibilities and church work. A disruption in the daily routine. A Sabbath pause. I laugh more at the Well than I do any other time of year.

One day, I am explaining our family's Sabbath experience and talking about the impact it's had, even though I still don't fully know what that impact is. I wrap up by saying, "And you know, if you want, I'd be glad to come to your churches and speak to Sunday school classes, retreat groups, or whatever and talk about Sabbath."

A friend pipes up, "Do you do birthday parties?"

I say, "Well, sure, but I don't juggle."

A pause.

"Oh, geez," I laugh. "I thought you were asking me to speak at a birthday party!"

After the group's laughter subsides, I continue. "Yes, if our children are invited to a birthday party on the Sabbath, we generally honor that. It's a chance for our kids to celebrate the gift of that friendship, which feels very Sabbath-y. But we buy the gift ahead of time. Which usually means we end up with a gift card."

"Sabbath requires a bit of slacker parenting, in other words," someone chimes in. Exactly.

Some Sabbath practitioners I've read suggest a rhythm: one day a week, one weekend a month, and one week a year for Sabbath rest. Not everyone can do this. Economic issues make this out of reach for many folks—I'm thankful that my time at the Well, intense though it is, provides a Sabbath week of sorts. And I'm thankful that my continuing education budget from the church makes it happen.

But travel isn't a requirement for a week of Sabbath; in fact, travel can add unnecessary stress. I've taken note of the recent move toward "staycations" and wondered if there is a bit of Sabbath embedded in the practice. Staycations have a financial component: people want a way to have a vacation without taking on the financial cost of travel, to enjoy one's hometown in a way that one can't while working. But isn't that what Sabbath is about—delighting in the sacred ordinary that's always around us? Being grounded in relationships and in place? Staycations may be Sabbath's way of hiding in plain sight.

*   *   *

I get back from the Well late Friday night, too late to see the kids. I catch a cab from the Metro station and as I approach home, I take a deep breath and steel myself before walking in the house. I hate coming home to a messy house and will even tidy the house prior to a vacation to avoid it. But when Robert is on his own with the three amigos, all bets are off. I almost always come home to a wreck, and this time is no exception. There's mail piled up, dishes covering the counter, and the floor of the family room is completely obscured by toys. I remember the old *Simpsons* episode in which Marge and Lisa go on a trip and Homer and Bart flop onto the living room floor and make trash angels in all the clutter.

But that's not fair; Robert has worked full time, fed and bathed our kids, overseen the homework, driven the carpool, and more. The mess is nothing; I use my Looney Tunes hack and look past the clutter to picture my colleagues' faces and hear their laughter ringing in my ears. I smile and greet Robert with a huge hug and kiss. I'm grateful for the time away and realize that a mess is a small price to pay to be able to have the time for rest, recreation and study. Robert is a peach. But I know that tomorrow, Sabbath, I will be tempted to clean it all up.

"No White Tornado tomorrow!" Robert says. "We'll work together on the mess later. Let's just enjoy your being home."

Sabbath begins as it usually does, with the footfalls of little ones padding down the hall and children crawling into our bed. This time it's Caroline and Margaret. I go downstairs with them and snuggle on the couch and doze off while they watch *Curious George.*

And the mess? We do the minimal amount of tidying (dishes, clearing off the table, sorting the mail) and let the rest go. Instead we get reacquainted after my time away. I'm thankful that reentry doesn't involve running around doing errands but can consist of long games of UNO, which Margaret wins every time.

The next day is Mother's Day. I'm not sure what Robert and the kids have planned because the day takes an unexpected turn. While getting ready for church, I walk into the bathroom to find Robert cradling one of our cats, who suddenly cannot walk on his hind legs. He's had a couple of health problems, typical stuff for a sixteen-year-old cat. But this is different.

"What's wrong with Willy?" James asks.

Robert meets my gaze, and it's a hard, piercing look. The message, via telepathy: *This is it.*

I breathe. Unfortunately, I still have to go to church and lead worship. "Can you wait to take him to the emergency vet until I get home? I want to be there with him. I can call Mom to see if she can come this afternoon to stay with the kids while we go."

"I'll try—he seems like he's not in any pain. If it gets worse, I'll have to take him without you."

I head out to church with the kids while Robert stays home. Later I get a text that he's found a vet that makes house calls. I'm thankful that Willy will die at home, comfortable, and not in a place that is foreign to him.

And so . . . death comes to us in the form of a compassionate, soft-spoken man with a black bag filled with medication that will help our cat die painlessly. Our kids don't want to be there when it happens, so they go for a walk with my mother. Robert and I stroke Willy's tuxedo coat as his breathing slows, and stops.

Sabbath means "stop," and death is the final stop. When a loved one dies, whether friend, family or feline, the nonessentials fall away. The day becomes a blur of hugs, tears and long wordless silences. What it isn't is busy. Any chores we might have done seem trivial.

Eventually we tiptoe back to workaday life–laundry can't wait forever–and maybe that too is the way it should be. Life moves on, but with a different texture because of the loss.

The kids are sad all week. A few weeks before, we had a robin's nest appear on our living room windowsill filled with three perfect eggs. We watched them day by day, trying not to peek too much lest we disturb the mother bird. When they hatched, we were proud and excited, even as we worried about the neighborhood cats. Sure enough, one morning we woke up to find the nest empty. It was the morning after the little ones had learned to cheep. I tore the nest off the windowsill and brought it inside so the robin wouldn't make the same mistake again. The kids drew pictures of baby birds and put them inside the nest. Soon enough it was time to throw the nest away.

That's a lot of death for little ones all at once.

When the kids get weepy about Willy and the baby birds, I hug and comfort them. I say the usual things: "I know, it's hard. I'm sad too. He was a great cat." Then: "It's OK, Sabbath is coming." I'm startled at myself, but they nod; they don't find it a non sequitur. Sabbath is a space to grieve. Mommy travels, Daddy works late, pets die, but Sabbath is coming without fail. It's more than a time to recharge. Maybe it's the place we get healed, too.

* * *

The next week, Caroline and James both initiate Sabbath with the morning cuddle, and then I remember: presbytery meeting. I jump out of bed and get myself going, envious that everyone else will have a day at home.

I get home around 2:00 and the kids are stir crazy. There have been fights. Margaret wants to ride her bike in one cul de sac and James and Caroline want to ride down the street in another.

"Ah, the classic suburban conundrum," I muse with more than a little sarcasm.

"Let's get out of here," Robert says.

"What, you and me?" I joke. "OK, let's all go to Mason Neck with the bikes."

"We'll need to take two cars to get all the bikes and ourselves there."

"So? You guys have been stuck here all day. It's time for a change of scenery."

"They are in no mood," Robert says, and it sounds like he's not either.

"Great, then it can't get any worse. Might as well be somewhere pretty."

I throw together some snacks and water and toss insect repellent into the bag while Robert pumps tires and loads bikes. It's like a game of Jenga to get them to fit.

Mason Neck is a state park about twenty minutes from our house. As I follow Robert there in the other car, I realize that we have been to Mason Neck at least once a season during our Sabbath year. It has been a Sabbath space, a place where we've seen the slow shifting of time in the changing of the seasons: from fall color to monochrome white to a slow budding of spring to a deepening green.

James has insisted on bringing his tricycle rather than his two-wheeler with the training wheels. It wasn't worth it to fight that fight, but I discover that a tricycle is an enforced slowing down. I toddle down the bike trail with James while Robert zooms ahead with the girls.

"I can't see Daddy! Where's Daddy?"

"He's up ahead with Caroline and Margaret," I say. "If we keep going we'll catch up to them."

We repeat this conversation about half a dozen times before catching a glimpse of them through a clearing.

Later, Robert and I switch, and sure enough, James gets anxious when he cannot see me.

When it comes to theology, I don't have all the answers. But I'm a big believer in spiritual *practices.* I know that the rhythms of life that Jesus embodied and the patterns of his story are life-giving. I pray and serve and worship God, and those activities change me. Through them I learn how to be in the world. If I want to love, I act in a loving way, even if I'm grumpy. If I want to be a generous person, I give to others, even when I'm feeling stingy. And if I want to view time more abundantly, I practice Sabbath. And I go at a tricycle's pace.

We all pedal back to the cars, and I remove my bicycle helmet. The kids laugh because the padding in the ancient helmet has disintegrated and left a grimy black stripe on my forehead. Afterward we find a new barbecue place to have dinner—a departure from our Sabbath meals at home. That night when we give the kids baths, they leave a ring in the tub. I love it: you know you've had a good Sabbath when it leaves a residue.

Sabbath Hack: Do the Harder Thing

Years ago I read an article that said, "It's easier to do what's hard than what's easy." This fortune-cookie paradox has become one of our axioms of parenting. Here's what it means to me: it's easier in the long run to put in a little extra effort and energy up front than to take the path of least resistance and hope everything works out.

Every few months, Robert and I get into serious laziness with going to the grocery store. Robert won't feel like making a list, or I won't feel like going except to buy the stopgap supplies: milk and bread. When faced with the decision between shopping or sitting on the couch, the couch always wins. The problem is that the easier thing (couch) takes a lot more effort in the long run. We spend days or weeks limping along on crappy fast food and mystery freezer containers crusted over with ice. Life would be so much better if we just up and went to the dang store. The harder thing (getting off our duffs and shopping) becomes easier (better meal options, happier family).

The concept applies well to children.

It's tiring, at the end of a long day of visiting parishioners in the hospital, to find the energy and creativity to pretend that the minivan is a space ship on the way to the space station (grocery store) to pick up supplies for our trip to the moon (our house). But as a result, the children view the errand with pleasure, not dread. And I find myself laughing too as I call out orders to First Officer Caroline, Lieutenant Margaret, and Sergeant James: "Oh no, we're turning into the asteroid belt! Let's make sure we don't get hit."

It's hard to find energy to clean up and organize the kids' toys. But it becomes the easier thing in the long run because then the kids can find what they need without asking me every five minutes to help them hunt for something. (Yes, there is a self-serving purpose here.)

It's a pain to assemble snacks or water bottles when we leave the house, but it's easier than enduring a hundred pleas for water when none is available.

And it's better to load up the car and head to Mason Neck and see if a change of scenery can reset cranky children than to tiptoe around their volatile little moods and hope that through some miracle, they will snap out of it on their own.

It's true that too much planning can become draining. We can make the easy things hard. But a little extra effort, a little extra kindness, and a little extra patience make a huge difference in fostering a sense of connection and even beauty—which is what we seek in Sabbath and in life.

Sabbath itself is the harder thing that becomes the easier thing. It takes no resistance to go with the flow and be reactive to the demands always pressing on us: cell phones, e-mail, urges to be useful. But the harder thing—Sabbath—becomes the more effortless, life-giving thing in the long run.

The Work of Sabbath: Kindle No Fire

Abraham Joshua Heschel, who wrote extensively on Sabbath, talked about the prohibition against kindling a flame on the Sabbath but extended the rule beyond physical flame. He said, "Ye shall kindle no fire—not even the fire of righteous indignation." The idea is that, on one day, we should do our utmost to let go of the annoyance and anger—even anger at things we're justified in being angry at.[4]

Our trip to Mason Neck is about doing the harder thing, but it's also an attempt to extinguish the bickering that my children had been doing (and inflicting upon their undeserving father). Sometimes a change of scenery and activity are enough to snap them out of their funk.

What takes place under our family's roof also happens in the greater society. I am struck by how much of our public discourse kindles the fires of rancor and stokes them mercilessly. Many corners of our culture seem to thrive on fear, anxiety, and trumped-up controversies. These controversies are flogged on cable news stations and then inexplicably disappear, only to be replaced by the new issue du jour.

Technology only heightens this dynamic. Writing in the early 1950s, Abraham Joshua Heschel could not possibly predict a Twitterverse or a 24-7 news cycle, but his words are prescient: "The solution of [humankind's] most vexing problem will not be found in renouncing technical civilization, but in attaining some degree of independence from it."[5]

My digital Sabbath has given me a degree of independence from the conflicts and kerfuffles that too often carry the day.

On the surface, it would seem that extinguishing fires of anger and resentment on the Sabbath is impossible, or at least an exercise in denial. It's not like we can switch our emotions on and off. But when we stoke our own resentments and rages, we can lose all perspective about them; they become the largest things in the universe. When we take a day to step away from the rancors that often consume our common life, we are reminded that life is larger than them. God is larger than our emotions. This breathing room seems essential to a healthy life, whether we're plagued by anger at a family member or "those clowns in Washington."

The Presbyterian Church (USA), in which I am a pastor, recently changed its church's constitution regarding a controversial issue. There are people who are upset by this change and others who are elated; there's been a lot of ugliness and infighting over the decades.

The church's constitution, like the U.S. Constitution, is changed through affirmative votes in the presbyteries (regional bodies). I remember the night that the final presbytery voted yes on the constitutional change. The commissioners–elders and pastors–cast their votes by secret ballot, and then they did something unexpected.

They put their meeting on hold, and while the votes were being counted, they had a meal together. Those of us who were following the meeting announcements on Twitter were dumbfounded: How can they delay letting us know the outcome? Don't they know that the world is watching?

But of course, that was the point. Whatever the result, their meal together was a testimony that they were brothers and sisters in Christ. The time would come for celebration on the part of some and lament and protest on the part of others. But during the meal, they kindled no fire. It was a Sabbath moment.

*　　*　　*

It's Memorial Day weekend, and once again, the three-day weekend throws us off our routine. We take lots of time for rest and play, but these moments are distributed throughout the weekend, not grouped onto a single day. I miss the long, uninterrupted time to sink into Sabbath as a family. But I like the whimsy and joy that come woven into the three busy days: little-kid cuddles, a movie, an impromptu campout in the backyard, homemade ice cream.

I wonder what will happen when our experiment ends. Will we continue to take a full day of Sabbath? Or will we feel adept enough that we can sprinkle a little Sabbath into our regular routine? Or will Sabbath slowly, sadly end?

11

June

I'll put brown sugar on my bread this time,
then go lie around by the water pump,
where the grass is very green and soft,
soft as the body of a red-winged blackbird.
Imagine, a blue silo to stare at,
and Mother not coming home till dark!

—DAVE ETTER[1]

I've been on a campaign against JOY for many years.

JOY is a mnemonic that's popular in some Christian circles. It stands for "Jesus first, others second, yourself last." The key to JOY, the saying goes, is to put God first, to serve others and to not be selfish and self-centered. And I respect those for whom a clear hierarchy of God/others/self works. Studies have shown that volunteering and serving others increases our own feelings of happiness and satisfaction.

But I have seen JOY backfire in tragic ways, often among women. I see it in their faces and bodies, wrung out like a dirty dishrag. They give and give and don't know when to stop. Like Moses before his intervention with Jethro, these folks have bought into the Messiah Trap, the idea that other people's needs are always more important than their own. Frankly, sometimes they are. But not always.

I knew a woman—I'll call her Rita—who grew up with that message. Many years ago I led a women's retreat on self-care and Sabbath and specifically called out JOY, which struck me as too simplistic and possibly destructive. Rita argued with me. "I love the

JOY thing. My grandmother taught it to me. I'm sorry, but too many people are counting on me. What you're saying isn't that simple."

I nodded, agreed that it wasn't simple, and let it go.

Some time after that, Rita's health started to fail. Some of us began checking on her, alarmed by her rapid weight loss and disheveled appearance. She put us off, insisting that everything was OK and refusing to face whatever was happening to her until it was too late. She passed away in her midfifties.

I was deeply grieved to hear Rita had died. Somewhere in my sadness, I remembered JOY. And . . . I wonder, that's all. Our bodies are intricate organisms. As with my father, I would never presume to declare inadequate self-care as a sole cause of someone's death. But the problem with putting others first is that there are seven billion "others" in the world. The need is always greater than we can meet. When does it end?

It ends when we see that Jesus' command to love our neighbor as ourselves doesn't work unless we remember the "ourselves" part. *Love your neighbor as [you love] yourself.* The words are missing grammatically but are necessary spiritually. When we love someone, we don't put their needs last. We don't give them the crumbs of our attention and care. We can't always put the person first—it's a dance, this business of love—but we certainly can't always put them last and expect that behavior to convey love. Even if the "someone" is ourselves.

Augustine wrote centuries ago that God loves each of us as if there were only one of us.[2] Maybe in our celebrity, look-at-me culture that leans toward narcissism, it's dangerous for us to live these words every day. But certainly it's enough to believe it one day a week, nestled into the greater spiritual context of Sabbath. We aren't loved because of what we do. And we aren't loved in *spite* of what we fail to do. We are loved because God is love.

We are loved, full stop. And so *we* can stop.

*   *   *

June is the month that school ends and summer begins. We'll see how our Sabbath experiment changes—or deteriorates—over the summer. We're traveling a lot, including family vacations, which will be fun and restorative. But vacations aren't Sabbath time, exactly. Traveling with kids requires effort and more than a little vigilance.

Has everyone gone to the bathroom at the rest stop? Are we well stocked on snacks? Are we going to give in to the demands for DVDs in the car? Vacations can be big fun, but they aren't always restful, what with sightseeing, sleeping in strange beds, and staying up past bedtime. Thankfully we are past the baby/toddler stages when we need to worry about unprotected power outlets and staircases without baby gates, but the fact is, there is no vacation from parenting.

"One thing at a time," Robert says. "We've still got to get through the end of school."

* * *

The tech Sabbaths have continued since I first began them in February. I began by unplugging for the weekend; now I extend it through the end of Monday. I am now off the computer for three days and on for only four. I continue to peek at e-mail in case work emergencies arise, but I do not respond to nonurgent messages. (Robert, for his part, has been on his smartphone less as well, though he's comfortable moderating his behavior as opposed to abstaining altogether.)

I can feel my thinking change on those days. When I first started, I was often twitchy and nervous. Now I look forward to the powering-down moment.

I remember a long road trip with some college friends a couple of years after graduation. We took two cars and borrowed a couple of CB radios so we could communicate with one another. (Remember those?) The radios were invaluable for coordinating bathroom stops and meals. And it was great fun; our games of Twenty Questions are the stuff of legend.

Midway through the second day of the trip, my friend Jay, who was driving the other car, abruptly said, "I'm going to turn off the CB for a while." We asked him about it at the next stop, and he said, "I love you guys . . . but it was starting to feel like too many people in the car."

Now, in the age of the Internet, I understand exactly how he felt. Between Facebook, Twitter, blogs, and news sites, sometimes there are way too many people in the car.

Friday nights, I turn off the computer. I even delete the Facebook application on my phone so that I won't log in on reflex. (It's easy enough to reinstall it on Monday night.) Many books about

Sabbath recommend a series of rituals that mark the putting away of work: setting aside briefcases, tidying papers, even shoving projects into a closet and out of sight. The powering down of the computer, with its little flicker and sigh, has become a spiritual trigger for me—I feel myself start to shift in attitude.

Many years ago someone shared with me the prayer from the New Zealand prayer book: "What has been done has been done; what has not been done has not been done; let it be."[3] It is now my pre-Sabbath prayer as I set everything aside, including the constant flow of information, news, and entertainment that is the Internet—the city that truly never sleeps.

Some friends, who hardly ever use the computer, don't see the significance of a tech Sabbath. "Big deal: I don't use the computer anyway." Well, I do, and I love technology. I genuinely enjoy my interactions on Facebook; it's a great source of information, support, and friendship. But I like the expansive feeling of being unplugged and untethered as well.

I feel like when I unplug, I am cultivating what singer-songwriter Peter Mayer calls a "million year mind." Tech Sabbath allows us to think more slowly but also more broadly. We are not "blown about" by every byte of data, to paraphrase one of the letters of the early church (Eph. 4:14).

And Sabbath should be a time for deep, unhurried rumination. Even our kids are starting to get to a place beyond gadgets. They hardly ever ask to watch television anymore on that day. I don't know that they're thinking deep thoughts, but they are better able to manage their restlessness and find things to do rather than ask for television at the first sign of discomforting boredom.

Some people are wary at the idea of a tech Sabbath: "Aren't you afraid of missing something? I couldn't do that." But my practice is a testimony as much as anything else: I do not need to comment on or "like" everything that happens in the world. Most stuff I don't even need to know about. The important things will come to me later or in some other way.

I am not alone in my unplugging; there is a larger shift in our culture, too. After several years of media and technological prolif-eration, people are starting to fight back, or at least becoming more thoughtful about their Internet use. Every week I see new books and articles about the benefits of disconnecting; many of these use the word Sabbath or sabbatical. One group is even selling cell phone "sleeping bags" to remind people that it's OK to let the buzzing gadgets rest every once in a while . . . or once a week, if you prefer. The group, wonderfully enough, is called Sabbath Manifesto, "a group of Jewish artists in search of a modern way to observe a weekly day of rest. The group are all members of Reboot, a nonprofit group designed to 'reboot' the cultures, traditions and rituals of Jewish life."[4] Hallelujah.

*   *   *

"Is this about the Ten Commandments?" someone outside the church asks me. "Are you taking Sabbath because you're commanded to do so?"

Yes and no. We're not very motivated by the *commandment* aspect of the Ten Commandments—perhaps we should be, but we don't observe Sabbath in order to follow the rulebook. Instead we are compelled by the idea that Sabbath can be a beneficial practice, and of course, that's why God offers it to the people along with the other nine commands. The children's ministry at a church I used to serve called the Ten Commandments the "ten best ways to live."

I've noticed that seven of the commandments are prohibitions *against* something (lying, murdering, committing adultery) and three are phrased in a positive, affirmative way. Seven say "don't"; three say "do." And all three of the "do" commands connect to Sabbath in some way.

First, we are called to honor God: commandment one says you shall have no other gods before God (Ex. 20:3). You shall affirm God alone; when other things try to take the place of God in your life, you shall remember that there is only one God and put everything else in its proper place. Sabbath helps us do this because we put away being useful and affirm that we are not in charge of our own lives.

Another affirmative command is to honor family. Specifically, "honor your father and your mother" (Ex. 20:12). I realize this commandment is problematic for many people whose parents did not treat them in ways that were very worthy of honor. In addition to its literal meaning, I read the commandment as an urge to be aware of where we've come from, to honor our past. Again, Sabbath helps us do this with its deep emphasis on family. Sabbath has traditionally been a communal practice that connects us with our roots—not only our father and mother and family of origin, but our spiritual families, people of faith who've gone before us and who have observed the Sabbath rhythm for countless generations.

A third affirmative commandment, of course, is to honor time: that is, to remember the sabbath day, to keep it holy (Ex. 20:8–11). This command helps us with the other two. All three, at the core, are about remembering–remembering who God is, remembering where we've come from, and remembering the gift of time. But remembering is not solely a mental exercise of recall. To remember is also to re-member, to put the pieces of our lives back together. Sabbath feels this way . . . sometimes. Other times–more often perhaps–it's enough to see the pieces in disarray on the floor and trust that all will be well.

*   *   *

A Saturday Sabbath in early June finds us in downtown DC with Margaret and James while Caroline plays at a friend's house. We are wandering with no plan. Over the years we've done plenty of tourist stuff in the city. This time, we are fascinated to see where a five- and three-year-old take us. At the World War II memorial, the signs caution us not to put our feet in the fountain, but the crowd can't resist and neither do we. Then we walk on toward the reflecting pool opposite the Lincoln Memorial, where there are ducks. I guess my kids gravitate to water. I am loving the aimlessness of seeing what catches their fancy next. It's as close as I will come to seeing the world through their eyes.

Meanwhile Robert is looking over his shoulder at the gray clouds on the horizon, fiddling with his phone, and mumbling about checking the radar. We hadn't brought umbrellas. I find myself almost rooting for a sudden shower. Isn't that the stuff of great kid memories? But that's the rub with technology now. You don't ever have to be caught in the rain.

I want to keep going, not change our plans. I want to make a run for it if it starts to rain: "Eh, relax, it'll be fine," I tell him. We compromise by walking to the National Museum of American History, where we can let the kids set the agenda once again without getting stuck in a gully washer.

"I think we've switched personalities," I say to Robert that night. "I'm usually the one who's worried about a sudden rainstorm. You're the spontaneous one. What gives?"

"I don't know. I guess I wanted to have a fun, relaxing day without any drama," Robert confesses.

As we talk, we realize that as much as we see ourselves as equal partners in our marriage, we have very different roles as parents during the week. We go where our gifts are: it's my job to keep the family operation in good working order—scheduling the appointments, checking the homework. Once Sabbath arrives, this household manager needs to rest: whatever happens, happens. By contrast, Robert works long hours during the week and is around the kids less, so on the weekends, he wants to make the most of those interactions, soaking up the time with us. If there are ways to minimize drama, he'll take it, even at the expense of spontaneity.

Seeing how differently we approach the Sabbath, even at this stage of the game, is a revelation. After ten months, we're still figuring things out.

* * *

With the end of school comes the beginning of swim team for Caroline.

Caroline has friends with older siblings. One afternoon she comes home from a playdate with this report: "They have a lot of trophies at their house."

And they do—swimming, soccer, basketball. They are an accomplished family. Our house, on the other hand, is trophy-free, except for last summer's swim team participation award given to everyone on the team.

I wonder what a continued emphasis on Sabbath will mean for the family trophy case. There's nothing in Sabbath that prohibits drive and achievement, of course. But Sabbath signifies a downshift, a deliberate choice not to jam our schedule full of activities. Fewer activities, fewer trophies.

I imagine us continuing Sabbath when the kids are older, when the tug of activities pulls on them even harder as they develop their own interests. Will they think about Sabbath time as an impediment? Or will they cherish a time to go at their own pace and follow their own desires and delights? Will they resent us for putting limits on their time? Or will this rhythm become ingrained in them?

The swim team practices each morning in the summer, with meets on Wednesday nights and (uh-oh) Saturday mornings. Last year was Caroline's first on the team, and she didn't swim the Saturday "A" meets, which are for the strongest swimmers. She is a dedicated and passionate swimmer but not particularly fast. This is OK with me. "Is it bad that I'm rooting for no Saturday meets?" I joke to Robert, wincing at what time we'd have to get up and out of the house. And Caroline is the dreamer, the introvert who gets energy from being at home, reading, playing in her room, and riding bikes with friends. The lack of Sabbath would affect her, no doubt.

Sure enough, Caroline comes home from Friday practice with instructions to report to the next day's meet. She's excited and nervous. I'm thrilled for her—it will be a great experience. But I do feel a small twinge of sadness because this is how it starts. Sabbath is easier when the kids are little. And then they grow up. They must; it's what we want for them. But there is loss.

I talk to friends, a husband and wife who have older kids. Their household is a well-oiled machine, powered by a monster calendar and frequent phone calls and texts between the parents to make sure that each kid is at the right practice or game. "I'm not looking forward to that," I say in a moment of honesty. The husband pipes up with great sincerity: "Oh no, these times are really great too! To see your kids mature and grow up . . ." his voice trails off. I look forward to that, but I am feeling fiercely protective of our family's Sabbath. I feel we've gotten closer over the course of this year.

On Saturday, Robert takes Caroline to the meet while I stay home with the other two. Margaret, James, and I have a lovely morning at home; they construct a makeshift replica of the Dawn Treader, the ship from the Narnia books, out of blankets and chairs. But our play is tinged with a little grief on my part that our family is changing, Caroline is growing up, and this Sabbath experiment may be living on borrowed time.

These melancholy feelings are interrupted by a text message from Robert: "Caroline got a blue ribbon in breast stroke!"

I whoop and share the news to Margaret and James. Margaret begins jumping up and down. (James follows suit; he has no idea what a blue ribbon is, but why should that stop him from celebrating?) Margaret, who encounters and processes the world through art, dashes into the other room to make a card for the victor. In an instant, my mind shifts from sadness over the changing rhythms of our family to thoughts of *Oh my gosh, she's good. What do we do? I never thought I'd have a jock in the family. I'm clueless!* While Margaret asks me to spell "congratulations," I break my tech Sabbath and turn on the computer, poking around for swim programs that meet during the school year. I am quickly stunned by the sticker shock and gasp when I see that some teams practice at 4:30 in the morning. I close the laptop with a sick feeling. I'm sure they're fantastic, but I don't want that for my kid.

Caroline comes home tired, sun-kissed and clutching her ribbon. I find out more information about her victory: she wasn't the first to touch the wall, but all the other swimmers in her age group disqualified, so she was awarded a blue ribbon. *Yeah . . . that's more like a Dana,* I think with a smile. I tell her the story of entering a 5K race as a teenager, completely unprepared. I received the blue ribbon for my age group because I was the only one who entered. But I am quick to add: a victory's a victory, and this is one to be proud of–she herself disqualified in the same event a week ago, so she's improving, and that's what matters.

Perhaps we don't need to jump into action to nurture the next Natalie Coughlin. Maybe we can help her enjoy her summer of swimming, improve her times, have fun and learn good sportsmanship and teamwork, and see what happens next.

Later I confess my frenzied Googling to Robert: "It's amazing how quickly I went from sadness over the end of Sabbath to researching ways to *add* things to our schedule."

Clearly we're not immune from the achievement bug that's so epidemic here. Parents want their children to play and be kids, but they also want them to be enriched, to have every opportunity to succeed. And when these two things conflict, people choose the latter. This mind-set is part of the air we breathe here. One of the neighborhood mothers has talked to me very earnestly about the importance of kids' "building their résumés."

Her children are in elementary school.

Caroline is eight. I don't want her to build her résumé. I want her to build a sense of adventure . . . and a sense of herself, her gifts, her limitations, and her strengths. I want her to build memories.

Later that day, the girls go down the street to play with friends. I later learn they were digging for earthworms. I go upstairs to take a nap and wake up to the sound of shrieks through the bedroom window. Suddenly I feel a presence next to me. Margaret is by the bed: "Mommy, Daddy is making water balloons with regular sized balloons! They're huge! Come on!"

Maybe they're not growing up yet. I get up–time to make a memory.

The Work of Sabbath: Letting Go

Over the course of this year, we've played with many different ideas of what makes the Sabbath a day set apart. We've seen that Sabbath can mean abstaining from work—that is, not changing one's environment—but it can mean many other things. Sabbath can mean simple delight, or it can mean doing one's regular activities at a slower, more deliberate pace. Sabbath can mean a focus on authenticity or on saying yes as much as possible. Another Sabbath invitation is a basic one that touches many of these elements but also stands alone: to let go.

Sometimes when I am leading worship, we will do a ritual of letting go as part of the prayer of confession. I ask people to open their hands in front of them, palms up, and I say: "Picture yourself holding something in their hands that you need to let go of. Imagine what that item feels like. Maybe it's heavy, large, or prickly. Or maybe it's a precious thing, but it needs to be given back to God or the universe, because holding onto it is making you unhappy. (For example, we may be concerned for a loved one in crisis whom we are unable to help—it may help us to let that stress go.)"

After they have imagined whatever it is they're holding, I encourage them, if they can, to close their hands firmly and feel how rigid their bodies get, how tiring it can be to cling to things so tightly. I do the gesture along with them and can feel my knuckles getting white and the muscles in my arm trembling ever so slightly.

Finally, I ask them to open their hands slowly and breathe, offering that situation or concern to God as they understand God.

This practice is a ritual and a prayer. As such, it doesn't "make it all better." But it does signal, in body and mind, an intent to let the burden go and to move on, even though moving on is a continual process. As Anne Lamott puts it, "Everything I've ever let go of has claw marks on it."[5]

Caroline's first Saturday meet with the "A" swimmers is only the latest reminder that our kids are growing up. We are ecstatic to see who they are becoming. They're sharp and sweet, strong and funny. They're obviously ours yet each completely themselves. But letting them go, bit by little bit, isn't easy. Sabbath has helped this letting-go process in a small way by providing a weekly pause. Time doesn't stop on that day, but having a day to stop our doing in favor of being has enriched our lives spiritually. We cherish as we let go.

This business of letting go has flowed to the rest of the week as well. I've started letting go more, whether it's leaving something unsaid or looking at the day's to-do list and deliberately removing something from it. I don't mean that I work diligently throughout the day and then look at the leftovers each evening and say, "Oh well, maybe tomorrow." I'm letting something go *preemptively*–looking at a task, good and worthwhile, and saying, "I'm not even going to try to accomplish that today."

I've always been drawn to the idea of the "Persian flaw," which is the practice of rug makers to include an intentional mistake in their creations. They do so because only God is perfect. The Persian flaw is as an act of devotion and humility.

I think of "letting something go" in the same way. One of the most important materials at my disposal is time, and after many years of ministry and motherhood, I've gotten pretty skilled at utilizing it. Sometimes too skilled. I'm trying to make time my friend again–a real friend, not the friend I only call when I need something. So making a conscious decision to let go is my Persian flaw. It's an act of devotion and humility.

The poetry of the creation story (Gen. 1) is very linear, very coherent: this category of stuff on day one, a completely new set of things on day two, and so on . . . rest on day seven. Nothing rolls over on the almighty to-do list: *Ooh, I plumb forgot to create asteroids . . . better get it done first thing tomorrow!* This kind of coherence is beautiful but infuriatingly beyond us. We will never measure up to the creation poem, so why even try? Letting one thing go each day is a way of acknowledging that perfection will always be beyond me. It also helps me find a little bit of Sabbath each day.

* * *

The question comes to me in response to a blog I've written about Sabbath. A mother of elementary-age kids writes, "Sabbath is more tiring than rejuvenating. I spend the day before getting ready for it, and the day after cleaning up from it. I just try to take some time each day instead of having a full day of Sabbath."

I would have said the same thing last September. It felt that way to me as well. But after more than nine months, I don't feel more stressed the next day with having more to do. I feel less stressed because I took time to truly rest: real rest, not the minimum amount of rest to gear up and be productive again.

Daily Sabbath time does seem to work for some people, and I do some of that too. Who am I to say what's right? But for me at this stage, snippets of Sabbath feel inadequate without a longer stretch of time each week or so. I end up feeling like Lightning McQueen in the Pixar movie *Cars*, making a much-needed pit stop but cutting it short: "No tires, just gas!" If I keep that up, I'm going to have a blowout.

On the other hand, the Sabbath isn't really about rest and rejuvenation at its core. That's sometimes a by-product but not the primary purpose. The primary biblical purpose as I see it is to put away the idol of control and power and a sense that we run the show. We do not. Are we really so very indispensable that we have to be "on" every single day of our lives except vacation, sickness, and when we just plain crash?

In that sense, Sabbath reminds me of tithing, another challenging scriptural practice that involves giving a tenth of one's money away to charity or the church. People who tithe do it as an act of faith that God provides what is needed. And they find, time and again, that they have what they need. Sabbath feels like a "time tithe" to me.

12

July

When we breathe, we do not stop inhaling because we have taken in all the oxygen we will ever need, but because we have all the oxygen we need for this breath. Then we exhale, release carbon dioxide, and make room for more oxygen. Sabbath, like the breath, allows us to imagine we have done enough work for this day. Do not be anxious about tomorrow, Jesus said again and again. Let the work of this day be sufficient.

—Wayne Muller[1]

Summer is a mixed bag in the Dana house. There are trips to the pool, late evenings of bike riding and sidewalk chalk, and the jangling tune played by the ice cream truck down our street every night. (Summer also means needling requests for popsicles.)

As always in the summer, there is yard work. Our string trimmer self-destructs one weekend, and Robert spends a sabbath day repairing it with replacement parts he ordered online weeks ago that have been sitting in a box in the hallway. I begin to remind him that it's Sabbath until I remember the firewood rack in January. He spends all week in an office, so tinkering is restorative for him. (Besides, the sidewalk in front of our house is half as wide as it should be, what with all the grass's raggedy encroachment on the pavement.)

Things slow down at church in the summer, which means a little more discretionary time to be with the kids. But summer is a difficult time for working parents. With children out of school, many of us cobble together childcare in the form of day camps, trips to see grandparents, and time off from work to be with the kids. It is not the skipping, barefoot time of my own childhood, and I need an air traffic controller to help me keep track of where everyone's supposed to be week after week.

This month I read an article lamenting that children don't have time to daydream and watch the clouds float by in summer, so busy are they with camps and enrichment activities. This article should be right up my alley—in fact, this argument has been part of our impetus to do Sabbath—but I feel my hackles go up instead. Many of us schedule our kids' summers because they're out of school and both parents work outside the home. It's not a plot to rob them of their childhood; it's a financial reality. I realize how many economic issues are tied up in how we spend our time. I cross my fingers in hope that my appreciation of Sabbath has never tipped over into dismissiveness of those who simply cannot take a daylong Sabbath for financial reasons.

It was this month, July, that Robert and I made our trip to Iona a few years ago. That's where the seed for Sabbath was planted, though that seed didn't do much growing until last year when our experiment began in earnest.

I remember our last night and morning on the island. Robert and I stayed up way too late talking while we packed our things—we were excited about this new Sabbath focus. We were leaving early the next morning with the rest of the group from our church. The following day I stumbled down to breakfast in the dining hall of the abbey where we were staying. I was still occupied with my thoughts and the previous night's conversation. While buttering some toast, I greeted another groggy person from our church group who said, "Boy, I could hardly sleep last night, thinking about all the connections." This woke me up a bit, and I wondered what kind of soul-searching *he'd* been doing. "Yes!" I said. "This place really works on you, doesn't it?"

He furrowed his brow, and I realized he'd been thinking about the upcoming day's travel back to the mainland, a complicated journey involving two ferries, a bus, and a train. The connections . . . not the *connections*.

Whenever I'm thinking too much, that story provides a gentle knock upside my head. Getting from point A to point B is enough of a puzzle sometimes in this life. No need to make it more complicated than that.

The Work of Sabbath: Play without Purpose

Back in May, while I was with my friends at the Well, we heard seminary professor Cindy Rigby make a presentation about the theology of play. She argued that play is vital to our spiritual lives and necessary for a healthy understanding of God.

Cindy told us about an event some years ago where she was asked to speak. When she proposed the theology of play as her topic, the event planners balked. *These are serious times we live in,* they said. *People are out of work; we are a nation at war. Play seems frivolous, a luxury we can't afford.*

Fine, she thought. So she tweaked the titles of her presentations to be more palatable to the organizers and went ahead and presented the play stuff under these new headings. We applauded her playful deviousness.

We all know people who are "too important to play." These people will tell you that, like the apostle Paul, they've put away childish things (1 Cor. 13:11). What a shame. It's when things are at their most dire that play becomes necessary. As Cindy spoke, I could see connections between play and Sabbath, especially the ways we need each and resist each.

Folks who study social interactions have argued that an unwillingness to play, or an inability to do so, is a symptom of an unhealthy or anxious system. Rabbi Edwin Friedman, a guru in the area of family systems, wrote that anxiety keeps people pessimistic, to the point that it becomes almost impossible for folks to reorient themselves toward positive change. A lack of playfulness contributes to a pessimistic orientation.[2]

By contrast, play helps people move into positive solutions and attitudes. Play encourages people to think creatively. And the best play for achieving these results is purposeless play, in which there's no product in mind or destination to reach.

Sadly, there's not much in scripture suggesting play as a God-approved activity. So much of the biblical story seems dreadfully earnest. But is it really? The best play has an element of surprise to it, and the outcome of play is ultimately beyond our control. I can think of few themes that resonate with the gospel story more than surprise and lack of control. Jesus does things in a way that suggests to me that, while he took his mission seriously, he also knew how to take himself lightly. His sparring with the Pharisees suggests a playful mind, even though the topics were deeply serious to his hearers.

His parables defy easy explanations and often end with a twist that expands his listeners' understanding of the reign of God. And the story of Jesus' resurrection is the ultimate "Yahtzee!" to all the powers that would seek to destroy him.

At any rate, play is a Sabbath-approved activity. Our family has played a lot this year. Robert has played with malted barley, hops, and yeast to brew beer, with a different result each time. I have played with some of the same ingredients as I've made bread, some of which turned out well, some of which didn't. We have played with Skip and Draw Four cards during rounds of UNO with our children. I can't measure the effects of such play, but I trust that something intangible is happening.

One of the planning teams at our church does something unusual as a committee: we play a board game together at each meeting. We take about twenty minutes and play Taboo, Cranium, or other light-hearted fun before getting down to business. It's a great bonding activity and helps loosen us up for fruitful conversation. (I can claim no credit for this idea—it was a team member's suggestion and the rest of us ran with it.)

A few months ago our team attended training with teams from other congregations that are looking at new ways to engage in ministry. More and more congregations are trying to move beyond the old 1950s way of being the church. While we were there, our team talked about the fun we've had playing games together and how it's become an important spiritual practice for us. The reaction was fascinating—people pushed back, hard. "Well, we'd all have to agree on the rules." "People would get so competitive." "It would get too complicated trying to keep score." (We don't keep score.)

One of the trainers heard this discussion, stopped everyone, and said, "Isn't it interesting how quickly we go from hearing a new idea to listing all the reasons why it won't work? And that's exactly why we're all here. To train ourselves to be open to new things in our religious communities."

Now board games are not the only way to be playful. For all I know, the naysayers are playful people who happen not to like games. But it was a striking moment. It led me to consider the times that I have been disdainful of purposeless play.

My point of anxiety is always around the issue of time. I'm the taskmaster that keeps this two-career, three-kid machine on track, after all. I like to play, but purposeless play makes me squirm. Yet the times that I have let Sabbath play and rest into my life have been the times in which I feel most creative, most productive, and most able to give and receive friendship and love toward others.

* * *

Our vacation in Maine will give us lots of time to play . . . but first we need to get there. We are planning to drive, and it's a two-day trip. In the past we have deployed DVDs strategically and liberally on road trips. I was a car DVD naysayer when they first came out—"I never had that as a kid!" I carped, ignoring the fact that my siblings and I were often bored out of our gourd on road trips and surely insufferable to our parents.

I have since been converted. DVDs are a godsend when we are clean out of ideas to entertain the kids, especially little ones who can't read or do other big-kid games. But movies in the car lead to their own problems—arguments over whose turn it is, constant requests to watch something else, or strung-out kids who need to be cajoled to look out the window every now and then.

This time, in a fit of playfulness, or mild insanity, I decide to leave the portable DVD player at home. We will eliminate the temptation altogether. I have seen my kids evolve in their use of screens over this year—they went from an inability to go a single sabbath day without television, to the rationed-out "token" system beginning in November, to going several Sabbaths in a row without even a mention of the television. So I think we can do this.

"It'll be fun," I grin a little too broadly as Robert and I load the car. I'm trying to convince myself as much as him.

"Maybe," he says, then adds, ever the reasonable one, "But let's load a couple of movies on our phones, just in case. We don't have to tell the kids." We also bring books on CD, some drawing books, and other car toys.

As we drive, we play a lot of the alphabet game, the "license plate" game (we even find an Alaska plate!), and I Spy . . . the kind of stuff Robert and I did as kids. There is plenty of bickering and boredom. James inexplicably gets stuck on the song "This Land Is Your Land" and demands to listen to it every hundred miles or so. But they do not whine about the DVDs. The option is off the table, so they don't even mention it. The five of us become our own entertainment in this enclosed space, along with the views whizzing by and our imaginations as we listen to the audiobooks. I make a mental note for next time: *leave the screens at home.*

The trip itself is a Sabbath experience. We are with family on a small lake in western Maine—no frills, no sightseeing, just a canoe, a small fishing boat, and lots and lots of time. But even after a year of eating, breathing, and sleeping Sabbath, I still fidget with this abundance of purposeless time. On our second evening, we have a freak rainstorm and lose power. I fret over the lack of electricity, which is ridiculous: our evenings in Maine consist of sitting on the porch, watching the lake, greeting folks as they stroll by, and listening for loon calls—in other words, nothing that a loss of electricity suddenly makes impossible. Still, I'm inwardly bugged—how long will this continue?

After the kids are tucked into bed, the adults ooh and aah over the last flashes of sunset that the rainstorm left in its wake. Robert nudges me from the next rocking chair: "What are you thinking about?"

"Honest to God, I'm thinking about the dirty dinner dishes piled up in the kitchen." He blinks. "I know. I need help."

I hear my mother's voice in my head: "Everything everywhere is all right already." Someday I'll believe it.

The power flickers back on a few hours later, prompting subdued cheers (don't want to wake the kids upstairs). I am grateful but embarrassed by how twitchy I was. I am thankful for this place.

And I'm thankful for the chance to get away, which I often take for granted. Indeed, paid time off is becoming more and more of a luxury in the United States. Organizations such as Take Back Your Time have been raising awareness for many years about overwork, overscheduling, and "time famine." The United States is alone among industrialized nations in not having a minimum annual leave statute; one recent survey found that only 57 percent of American workers had taken a week's vacation the previous year. Meanwhile, people who do not take regular vacations can suffer serious health issues. Vacations also benefit companies; workers come back from vacations more alert, rested, and creative.[3]

With the current economic crisis still looming, conversations about paid vacation leave take on a different tone. People who've been out of work for a long time are looking for *any* decent job; benefits such as vacation time are a secondary concern. But there's no denying that time off is wrapped up in justice issues—it's another way of separating the haves from the have-nots. And these issues are not new: Sabbath, after all, is connected to the people of Israel, who were slaves under Pharaoh's command. After their flight from Egypt, Sabbath became a sign and testimony that the people were free from the burden of constant work. Sabbath time, whether in weekly or week-long forms, is something I want for everyone—even though I too often let inconveniences like temporary power outages get in the way of my enjoyment of it.

* * *

The alarm goes off at 6 a.m., and I fumble around in the dark before remembering that I'm not home in Virginia waking up for a day of work. I'm in Maine, and today I'm climbing Mt. Washington in New Hampshire.

I pull on some clothes and tiptoe downstairs to find my mother-in-law and sister-in-law, hiking boots on, filling their backpacks with energy bars, water, and Band-Aids. I make myself a quick bowl of oatmeal and then add a banana and a dollop of peanut butter for good measure. Soon, we're off for the hour-long drive to the trailhead.

Climbing Mt. Washington is not a Sabbath activity by any sane definition. I can *perhaps* see it as a way of bringing my life into balance—our November "work of Sabbath"—since I live a largely sedentary, indoor life. Or perhaps it is a powerful example of cultivating novelty, as we found in January—I've hiked other trails over the years but nothing this strenuous.

But there's no getting around the fact that this hike will be hard work. The route we take is only four miles to the summit but involves a 4,000-foot elevation change, including a couple of hours of scrambling on large boulders near the top. It is also the culmination of several months of training. In February, I began a practice of running. I am slow as molasses, especially in my hilly neighborhood, but I figure the hills are as good a preparation as any for a mountain hike.

If I make it to the top in one piece, I will see it as a spiritual achievement—a triumph of Sabbath. I have wanted to get into better shape for years. Something always stopped me—pregnancy, nursing, laziness, busyness. I'd start a fitness program with great gusto and peter out. Or I'd achieve a goal, but without a new goal, I'd slide back into old habits.

Something changed this year. Somehow I hit upon the right attitude to start taking better care of myself physically. I can't say for sure that Sabbath made the difference. On the other hand, why not? Perhaps Sabbath provided the mental reset that allowed me to see physical fitness as doable in my crammed life. Sabbath is not only an exercise of the mind but a complete mind-body-spirit endeavor.

It's a hard climb for me, much harder than I'd imagined. I huff and puff at the back of our threesome, not so much the Little Engine That Could as the rickety caboose at risk of being decoupled and rolling back down the track. Meanwhile, we keep getting passed by lithe and tanned folks, telling each other their life stories as they pick their way up the rocks. It is a struggle for me even to gasp out a "Hello," let alone what I want to say: *I hate you and your impressive fitness level.*

Midway up the mountain, the glue comes undone on my right boot, and the sole goes flapping until I stop and cut it off with some nail scissors. (Why did we have nail scissors and not duct tape? And how could I not have checked the state of my ancient hiking boots before starting out?) Closer to the top, I lose the other sole. Thank goodness Mt. Washington has a way down the mountain via van and cog railway–there's no way I'm hiking down without traction on either boot.

As tiring as it is to reach the top, it is thrilling. My mother-in-law and I grab each other's hands and walk to the visitors' center, where our family waits for us–along with a bowl of clam chowder.

As I sip the steaming hot chowder, I feel surprisingly good. I remember the first long hike I ever did, a grueling nine-miler with Robert in the early years of our marriage (when I was in much worse shape than I am now, though fifteen years younger). We were camping in Colorado, and I recall that after the hike, we got back to our campsite with three urgent and competing needs: We were hungry and in need of a good meal. We were tired and desperate for a nap. And we were sweaty and gross, in need of a long hot shower. I spent a long moment feeling a desperate, silly paralysis: *I need all these things and I need them all RIGHT NOW.*

Many of us live strenuous lives, hiking to the very edge of what our bodies and spirits can stand. As one mother I know puts it, "There is no buffer. Our lives work smoothly until someone gets sick or the dishwasher breaks, and then all hell breaks loose." There's no space to absorb the unexpected. Even when everything is going well, it is challenging to assess what is the next right thing. If we tend to one area of our life, the other areas must wait patiently—or not.

But if the Colorado hike was a parable, so was Mt. Washington. I feel tired but invigorated. The hike was hard, but I was better prepared physically and spiritually. I paced myself, both beforehand and during the hike itself. I left myself more of a buffer so that I was not completely spent (it took us six hours, after all—about two hours longer than most people). I feel the experience guiding me to think about my life in a healthier way: *Look! You can achieve cool things while not pushing yourself to the absolute breaking point. You can leave some breathing space and not be exhausted all the time.*

I say a prayer of thanks for this little bit of grace and the lens of Sabbath, which allowed me to see it.

* * *

We return from Maine and head right into the height of the swim meets, which continue on their Saturday mornings. We adjust our Sabbath accordingly as much as possible—instead of the entire day on Saturday, we take the afternoon. It's less than we'd like, but better than nothing.

Later in July I have a writing getaway, which means Robert will be holding down the fort. Through all our comings and goings, Sabbath pokes through, primarily in the form of lazy afternoons at the pool and leisurely dinners on the deck. It is fortunate that we have more than ten months of experience under our belts; otherwise the practice would have gotten lost in the shuffle.

13

August . . . and Beyond

When the fiddle had stopped singing Laura called out softly, "What are days of auld lang syne, Pa?"

"They are the days of a long time ago, Laura," Pa said. "Go to sleep, now."

But Laura lay awake a little while, listening to Pa's fiddle softly playing and to the lonely sound of the wind in the Big Woods. She looked at Pa sitting on the bench by the hearth, the fire-light gleaming on his brown hair and beard and glistening on the honey-brown fiddle. She looked at Ma, gently rocking and knitting.

She thought to herself, "This is now."

She was glad that the cosy house, and Pa and Ma and the fire-light and the music, were now. They could not be forgotten, she thought, because now is now. It can never be a long time ago.

—LAURA INGALLS WILDER[1]

Sabbath continues this month, as it has each of the eleven months that preceded it: with flashes of beauty and intimacy inter-mixed with moments of boredom and irritation. The busyness of the weekends makes protecting Sabbath a challenge, and it will always be thus. We've decided to continue Sabbath beyond our Sabbath year but with a twist: we will take Sunday as our Sabbath, unless I have a church commitment on Sunday afternoon, in which case, we will take Saturday. We'll see how it goes; I expect we will reconfig-ure things as we go. I agree with the writer who said that we receive Sabbath as a gift in the same way that we might receive a musical instrument: the gift's value is found in what we do with it. We must continue to practice to take full advantage of it.[2]

All summer long I've been looking at the glass bottle that's been sitting on our kitchen counter. It's a deposit bottle that we bought from a dairy at the farmers' market in June–a special treat of chocolate milk. We get a dollar back if we return it, but we haven't been back to the farmers' market since then–it's only open on Saturdays. The bottle stands as a reminder that saying yes to something good has meant saying no to something else that's also good–namely, fresh produce and the chance to buy locally. (It's one of the nasty little secrets of the simplicity movement: simplifying in one area makes other areas complicated. It takes additional time to make a separate stop at the farmers' market. The produce at the grocery store may come from Chile, but it's right there with the canned goods and toothpaste.)

I try to "Looney Tunes" the bottle; like I do with other things left undone, I picture all the things we did instead. I imagine that bottle filled with memories of all we experienced together.

The bottle overflows: I cram it full of our many morning snuggles, and the time that Margaret shared at dinner that her "favorite thing about today" was that it was Sabbath. I throw in a piece of the Harry Potter world we made out of blocks. There's the beginning of a scarf made by Caroline. There are silly songs and Margaret finally learning to swim underwater. There are homebrews and countless trays of Bagel Bites.

And there are dreams about the future. Robert and I start making plans to take the kids to Iona someday, where the Sabbath experiment began. It will take countless machinations and considerable savings to make it happen. But I long for my children to stand on a beach littered with ancient stones, looking for the right ones to hold in their hand, to click in their pockets as they walk.

Sabbath Hack: Embrace Scarcity

Over the years, I've noticed a peculiar emphasis in the church on the language of abundance. Abundance is the idea that there is always enough, not necessarily for what we want but for what we need. God provides what God's people need, whether it is safe passage out of slavery, manna in the wilderness, or a promised land. Jesus, too, "came that they may have life, and have it abundantly" (Jn. 10:10). Love, justice, hospitality, peace–these are all hallmarks of the abundant life Jesus promises.

Abundance is a powerful counternarrative to a culture that likes to preach scarcity. Too often we are told that there is not enough for everyone. We must hoard what we have; we must be suspicious; we must claw our way toward the top, where there's only room for a privileged few.

Through its preaching on abundance, the church is able to expose the culture's proclamation of scarcity as the lie that it is. The reign of God that Jesus sought to preach, model, and inaugurate is not a winner-take-all system. The favored citizens in Jesus' beloved community are not the privileged and the wealthy but rather the poor, the down-and-out, the sick, and the outcast. In that sense, a theology of abundance is a vital and necessary message that we need to hear.

It's important to understand what abundance means here. We're used to thinking of abundance as surplus, but God's abundance, in this context, is really about a blessed "enough-ness": The extra money that comes your way right when you really need it. The phone call from a friend when you're at the very end of your rope. The delightful way there's always enough at a church potluck to feed everyone who shows up.

However, a theology of abundance only takes us so far. For one thing, the message can be corrupted into a pernicious gospel of prosperity. If God is wrapped up in notions of abundance, and we happen to have an abundance of wealth, then clearly our affluence is God's doing. God *wants* us to be rich. There are entire churches built around this corrupted gospel message.

But there is another danger in the theology of abundance, and that is an overly simplistic, sloganeering faith that papers over the very real limitations we run into every day. I have heard countless times in the church—and even preached myself—these kinds of messages: *There is enough. You have enough. You are enough. You do enough.* These messages are affirming, but when it comes to time, are they accurate?

Is there really enough time for those things that are truly needful? Do we really have enough time for the important stuff? If we take this abundance talk too far, the logical conclusion is this: if we find ourselves with something left undone, then it didn't need doing anyway. And if we're stressed out with more to do than we have time to do it, then that's *our* problem, because after all, God provides all the time we truly need.

The Sabbath can unwittingly play into this notion: some Sabbath practitioners will tell you that when you embark on a regular Sabbath practice, you will find that you have enough time for what was needed.

After a year of Sabbath, I think they are wrong.

I myself have come to reject the concept of time abundance. If God truly provides enough or even abundant time, then life becomes a puzzle to be solved. And it *can* be solved, provided we come up with the right configuration of pieces. Thinking about time this way, we are doomed to a life of anxiety, always chasing after the exact perfect balance of activities to fill our days. If God provides enough time for the important things in our lives, and we don't get them done, then we've failed to solve the puzzle, to find the right answer.

I see the theology of abundance as a game of Free Cell, the computer solitaire game. My father-in-law has won hundreds of Free Cell games over the years because he's tenacious and sharp and knows that almost every game of Free Cell can be solved. There is a solution if you work at it long enough.

But life is not a game of Free Cell. Sometimes life is old-fashioned solitaire, in which the ace you need is underneath the pile of face-down cards and there's no way of getting to it. I have a friend who's caring for a spouse with bladder cancer. His survival depends on a drug that has been unavailable for several weeks at a time—there are problems with the manufacturer that I don't fully understand. He may simply run out of time. A theology of abundance has little to say to them as they wait. A theology of "enough-ness" is not a comfort to the person who always thought there'd be more time with their loved one to say all the things that needed to be said.

I have found it much more liberating spiritually to embrace the idea of holy scarcity. There isn't ever enough time. Even when we strip away all the inessentials—even when we focus only on the things that are good and nourishing and important for ourselves, our families, and the world—there is still not enough time. But our hope is not in there being enough time but in there being enough grace to muddle through the scarcities of our days.

I remember clearly a day when Caroline was a toddler. I'd had a hard day; we were away from each other for most of the day while I worked and she played at daycare. That evening I'd spoken sharply to her over something that, in retrospect, was not worth such a strong response. Later, when I knelt by her bed to check on her before going to bed myself, it hit me: *That's it. That's all I had with her today. And there will be more days like this. It wasn't enough time. And the time I did have, I squandered.*

I'm sorry. Tomorrow will be better.

The note on the wall above my desk helps me remember: "Today is their childhood." Today and only today. That's what holy scarcity is.

Sometimes that scarcity makes my teeth itch. My firstborn child is halfway to *driving*, for Pete's sake. Other times that scarcity fosters a sense of urgency, an excitement to make the most of the little crumbs of time we've been given.

The fact is, abundance is boring. Video game makers know this. Robert tells me that from time to time game makers will design a game with unlimited lives, unlimited tools and resources—and people hate playing them. Where is the challenge, where is the fun in that? Time scarcity demands that we be creative. There isn't enough time. So how do we move as creatively through our days as we can?

After a year of Sabbath, we don't have the answer. But that's the question we continue to live with.

*   *   *

At the beginning of our Sabbath experiment, I ran across a quote from the twentieth-century Swiss theologian Karl Barth: "A being is free only when it can determine and limit its activity."[3]

I've thought all year about this definition of freedom. As parents of three young children, by this definition, Robert and I are not free. It was our choice to have them, of course. But it was a choice that involved giving up freedom.

We do not "determine our activity." The middle schoolers in our neighborhood trudge to the bus stop at 6:30 in the morning. If we stay in this neighborhood, my children will do the same. I don't relish the math of figuring out what time we need to rise in order to get preteens out the door at 6:30. Left to my own devices, I would not get up at that time. (As a pastor friend likes to say, "I don't even believe in God until at least 10 a.m.")

As for *limiting* my activities, I am able to do so but only somewhat. Sabbath has been an attempt to establish limits, but given how much negotiating and tweaking is required, it would seem that even my limits have limits.

As children get older, they generally do not require quite as much from their parents. Every day I think, "Today they are as dependent on me as they will ever be again." (Emotional needs can get more complicated as kids age, however; a friend of mine says, "They don't need you physically as much, but the *emotional* energy I spent helping my girls navigate adolescence was just as exhausting.")

So by Karl Barth's definition, I am not a free person and won't be for some time, if ever.

But then I remember, neither are my children.

One year later, I still have to drag them around on errands they don't want to do. Robert and I make the final decisions about family activities, extracurriculars, and vacations, and they are along for the ride.

But on one day a week, we *are* free. On Sabbath we are fellow travelers, parents and children, learning what it means to stop, reflect, breathe, and play.

It is ironic that we have experienced freedom by submitting to a restricting discipline like Sabbath. It seems impossible that restricting our freedom has only increased our feeling of freedom . . . but it has.

When I was in third grade, I played kickball for the first time. I was very aware that everyone else knew the rules except me. I watched the person before me kick the ball and run to first base and stop. All eyes were on me as I gamely stepped up to the plate.

Wonder of wonders, as the ball came rolling bouncily toward me, I drew back my foot at just the right time. The red ball made a hollow KANG as it sprang forward.

My team cheered as I ran for first. Safe!

And then I kept running. I made it to second, where I came face to face with . . . my teammate. "What are you doing?" the kid asked. "Why didn't you stop? We can't be on the same base. You're out now."

I didn't know the rules. And until I learned the rules, every game I played was a challenge requiring a mental conversation: *OK, she kicked the ball and it's rolling. That means they have to throw it to first so she can be out. That ball's flying through the air. So if someone catches it, the runner is automatically out. They didn't kick the ball after three tries, so they're out.*

By the time I got to fourth grade, I was ready for softball, which was like kickball in the mechanics of the game. By the time I was in sixth grade, I didn't have to think about the difference between tagging and throwing to the base. (I'll never understand the infield fly rule though.)

When you're learning to play a game, or watching one from the sidelines for the first time, the rules seem overwhelming. Everything seems too much for the novice: *I'll never get this.* But you keep learning the rules and the skills because you see joy in the playing.

Sabbath is like that. People say to me all the time, "I couldn't do that." But once they internalize the game, they can if they choose to.

When our family started keeping Sabbath, we spent inordinate amounts of time figuring out the boundaries of play. All day I would evaluate what we were doing: Work? Not work? I don't have those internal discussions that much anymore. Our definition of work shifts from time to time, and we make up our own rules. The field of play changes, too. But there are basic rules that do not change. Nevertheless, the rules don't feel confining because Sabbath is a game we want to play.

When I was in college, I had a long discussion with a Jewish friend about following the kosher laws. Having different dishwashers for different kinds of dishes seemed, frankly, bizarre to me. Why were there so many regulations, and how was that in any way a useful or fulfilling thing to focus on? She responded that obedience to the law was a joy, not a burden. It was a constant reminder of who she was and where she came from. And because the laws touched many aspects of life, she was able to receive those reminders at a lot of different times and places.

I get it now, because that tension between freedom and restriction is present in my tradition, too. The apostle Paul talks in Galatians about Christian freedom, and it's a paradox: "You were called to freedom, brothers and sisters; only do not use your freedom as an opportunity for self-indulgence, but through love become slaves to one another" (Gal. 5:13). True freedom, it seems, comes from participating in a particular pattern of life that seems restricting but is actually life-giving. There's something beautiful in giving oneself wholly to the game one has chosen.

The Work of Sabbath: The Healing of the World

I attended a retreat in rural Georgia many years ago at a retreat center run by Dominican sisters. I met with one of them and we got to talking about the practice of centering prayer, which is a deep, silent time of contemplation and listening for God. Practitioners recommend twenty minutes, twice a day. It's serious stuff.

My friend said, "There is a movement under way as more and more people learn about and practice centering prayer. The interest is growing. And we believe that if enough people take part in it, the whole world will change. We believe this kind of prayer can change the world."

I want desperately for her words to be true. I long to believe that millions of people at prayer, listening daily for God, can change things—that a warring people will cease their fighting, that generosity will prevail in a world that's often stingy and small. But my faith is weak sometimes.

Someone has called Sabbath the most radical sociopolitical invention in four thousand years. That person must have a faith that's more robust than mine. But that faith is enough to get me started. I picture people all over the world, keeping the Sabbath in their own ways, whether with candles and blessings on Saturdays, Christian worship and a slow leisurely afternoon on Sundays, or countless other variations. I see people picking up this book, or reading an article online, and making one small change that will allow a little gracious slack into their schedules. I imagine people shutting down the computer, stowing the iPhone, and looking their beloved in the eye with an attentiveness so true and dear that it startles them both. I see children teaching parents how to play again. I dream of congregations deciding not to add one more program to an already full schedule and instead giving people tools to embrace Sabbath in their own ways, in their own homes, in their own hearts.

I don't have illusions that Sabbath-keepers will ever be a huge group. But I love the audacity of my Dominican friend in Georgia. I like to think that maybe, as people persist in this practice, and others join them, the world will shift on its spiritual axis ever so slightly.

Notes

Chapter 1

[1] Israel Shenker, "E. B. White: Notes and Comment by Author," *New York Times*, July 11, 1969, accessed December 1, 2011, http://www.nytimes.com/books/97/08/03/lifetimes/white-notes.html.

[2] Michael Strassfeld, *A Book of Life: Embracing Judaism as a Spiritual Practice* (New York: Random House, 2002), 108.

[3] Blu Greenberg, *How to Run a Traditional Jewish Household* (New York: Simon and Schuster, 1983), 52.

[4] Ruth Perelson, *An Invitation to Shabbat: A Beginner's Guide to Weekly Celebration* (New York: UAHC, 1997), 10.

Chapter 2

[1] "Century Marks," *Christian Century*, May 2, 2006, http://christiancentury.org/article/2006-05/century-marks.

[2] Blu Greenberg, *How to Run a Traditional Jewish Household* (New York: Simon and Schuster, 1983), 31.

[3] Ibid., 40.

[4] Wayne Muller, *Sabbath: Finding Rest, Renewal, and Delight in Our Busy Lives* (New York: Bantam Books, 1999), 189–90.

[5] Abraham Joshua Heschel, *The Sabbath* (New York: Farrar, Straus and Giroux, 1951), 12.

Chapter 3

[1] Blu Greenberg, *How to Run a Traditional Jewish Household* (New York: Simon and Schuster, 1983), 26–27.

[2] Michael Strassfeld, *A Book of Life: Embracing Judaism as a Spiritual Practice* (New York: Random House, 2002), 120.

[3] Ruth Perelson, *An Invitation to Shabbat: A Beginner's Guide to Weekly Celebration* (New York: UAHC, 1997), 23.

[4] Abraham Joshua Heschel, *The Sabbath* (New York: Farrar, Straus and Giroux, 1951), 21.

[5] Greenberg, *How to Run a Traditional Jewish Household*, 75.

[6] Strassfeld, *Book of Life*, 107.

[7] Mary Oliver, "The Journey," in *New and Selected Poems, Volume One* (Boston: Beacon Hill, 1993), 114.

Chapter 4

[1] *Ferris Bueller's Day Off,* dir. by John Hughes (1986; Paramount Pictures, 2006 DVD).
[2] Blu Greenberg, *How to Run a Traditional Jewish Household* (New York: Simon and Schuster, 1983), 28.

Chapter 5

[1] Georg Weissel, "Lift up Your Heads, Ye Mighty Gates," in *The Presbyterian Hymnal,* trans. Catherine Winkworth (Louisville, Ky.: John Knox, 1990), 8.
[2] Rachel Rettner, "Study: Happiness Is Experiences, Not Stuff," March 5, 2010, http://www.livescience.com/6158-study-happiness-experiences-stuff.html.
[3] Abraham Joshua Heschel, *The Sabbath* (New York: Farrar, Straus and Giroux, 1951), 75.
[4] Judith Shulevitz, *The Sabbath World: Glimpses of a Different Order of Time* (New York: Random House, 2010), 24–26.

Chapter 6

[1] Carrie Newcomer, "Holy as a Day Is Spent," *The Gathering of Spirits,* Label: Philo, 2002.
[2] David Allen, *Getting Things Done: The Art of Stress-Free Productivity* (New York: Penguin, 2001), 179.
[3] Gretchen Rubin, *The Happiness Project: Or, Why I Spent a Year Trying to Sing in the Morning, Clean My Closets, Fight Right, Read Aristotle, and Generally Have More Fun* (New York: HarperCollins, 2009), 74.

Chapter 7

[1] Wayne Muller, *Sabbath: Finding Rest, Renewal, and Delight in Our Busy Lives* (New York: Bantam Books, 1999), 83.
[2] Judith Shulevitz, *The Sabbath World: Glimpses of a Different Order of Time* (New York: Random House, 2010), 5.
[3] David McRaney, "Extinction Burst," You Are Not So Smart, July 7, 2010, http://youarenotsosmart.com/2010/07/07/extinction-burst.

Chapter 8

[1] Patty Digh, *Life Is a Verb: 37 Days to Wake Up, Be Mindful, and Live Intentionally* (Guilford, Conn.: Skirt, 2008), 187.
[2] Frederic Brussat and Mary Ann Brussat, "Meister Eckhart," Spirituality and Practice, http://www.spiritualityandpractice.com/days/features.php?id=15347.
[3] Wayne Muller, *Sabbath: Finding Rest, Renewal, and Delight in Our Busy Lives* (New York: Bantam Books, 1999), 173.
[4] "The Wisdom of Tenderness," Jean Varnier, interview by Krista Tippett, *On Being,* December 20, 2007, http://being.publicradio.org/programs/wisdom oftenderness/index.shtml.

Chapter 9

[1] Debbie Blue, *From Stone to Living Word: Letting the Bible Live Again* (Ada, Mich.: Brazos, 2008), Kindle edition, location 1151.

[2] Barbara Brown Taylor, *An Altar in the World: A Geography of Faith* (New York: HarperOne, 2009), 7.

Chapter 10

[1] Wayne Muller, *Sabbath: Finding Rest, Renewal, and Delight in Our Busy Lives* (New York: Bantam Books, 1999), 3.

[2] Carmen Renee Berry, *When Helping You Is Hurting Me: Escaping the Messiah Trap* (New York: Crossroad, 2003).

[3] Abraham Joshua Heschel, *The Sabbath* (New York: Farrar, Straus and Giroux, 1951), 5.

[4] Ibid., xiv.

[5] Ibid., 28.

Chapter 11

[1] Dave Etter, "Marcus Millsap: School Day Afternoon," in *Alliance, Illinois* (Evanston, Ill.: Northwestern University Press, 2005).

[2] John R. Bodo, *Who They Really Were: Preaching on Biblical Personalities* (Lima, Ohio: CSS Publishing, 2000), 85.

[3] *A New Zealand Prayer Book* (New York: HarperOne, 1989), 184.

[4] Sabbath Manifesto website, http://www.sabbathmanifesto.org.

[5] Anne Lamott, "Loving Bush: Day 2," *Salon*, September 26, 2003, http://www.salon.com/2003/09/26/loving_bush.

Chapter 12

[1] Wayne Muller, *Sabbath: Finding Rest, Renewal, and Delight in Our Busy Lives* (New York: Bantam Books, 1999), 83.

[2] Edwin H. Friedman, *A Failure of Nerve: Leadership in the Age of the Quick Fix* (New York: Seabury Books, 2007), 63.

[3] "Take Back Your Time," http://www.timeday.org/right2vacation/care.asp.

Chapter 13

[1] Laura Ingalls Wilder, *Little House in the Big Woods* (New York: HarperTrophy, 1971), 237.

[2] Ruth Perelson, *An Invitation to Shabbat: A Beginner's Guide to Weekly Celebration* (New York: Union of American Hebrew Congregations, 1997), 57.

[3] Barbara Brown Taylor, *An Altar in the World: A Geography of Faith* (New York: HarperOne, 2009), 125.

TO DO

NEW...FRESH...

The Young Clergy Women Project (TYCWP) Series

Who's Got Time?
Spirituality for a Busy Generation
by Teri Peterson and Amy Fetterman

Where does a relationship with God fit into our 24/7/365 living? *Who's Got Time?* offers new ways to incorporate spiritual practices into the busy lives of generations X, Y, and beyond.

Print ISBN 9780827243057, $16.99

NEW

Seamless Faith
Simple Practices for Daily Family Life
by Traci Smith

Faith is learned when it is woven seamlessly into the fabric of everyday life. In *Seamless Faith*, author Traci Smith shares dozens of simple practices to equip families of all kinds with the tools they need for bringing faith home. Filled with easy-to-organize traditions, ceremonies, and spiritual practices for many of life's stressful and faith-filled moments, this is a resource parents will return to for years to come.

Print ISBN 9780827235342, $18.99

 **CHALICE** PRESS

1-800-366-3383 • www.ChalicePress.com
Ebooks also available

EVOCATIVE VOICES

The Young Clergy Women Project (TYCWP) Series

Making Paper Cranes
Toward an Asian American Feminist Theology
by Mihee Kim-Kort

This theological book engages the social histories, literary texts, and narratives of Asian American women, as well as the theological projects of prominent Asian American feminist theologians.
Print ISBN 9780827223752, $16.99

Any Day a Beautiful Change
A Story of Faith and Family
by Katherine Willis Pershey

In this collection of interrelated personal essays, Katherine Willis Pershey chronicles the story of her life as a young pastor, mother, and wife. *Any Day a Beautiful Change* will strike a chord with anyone who has ever rocked a newborn, loved an alcoholic, prayed for the redemption of a troubled relationship, or groped in the dark for the living God.
Print ISBN 9780827200296, $14.99

Bless Her Heart
Life As a Young Clergy Woman
by Stacy Smith & Ashley-Anne Masters

Comprising essays from young women clergy, this book is a reflection on the everyday realities of pastoral ministry for the young, female professional.
Print ISBN 9780827202764, $15.99

1-800-366-3383 • www.ChalicePress.com
Ebooks also available

The Young Clergy Women Project

is a network of the youngest ordained clergy
women, defined as those under forty. With more
than 650 members, we live across the United States
and around the world, and represent more than
two dozen denominations. We gather whenever we
can—regionally, at denominational events, at an
annual retreat, and online. TYCWP publishes new,
fresh and evocative articles every Tuesday and
Thursday written by members of our community
on Fidelia's Sisters, and we have partnered with
Chalice Press to publish a book series authored by
TYCWP members.

We do all this to provide members with new
professional and personal relationships and
opportunities to share their wisdom with their
peers.

Learn more about The Young Clergy Women Project
online at youngclergywomen.org.

the young
clergy
women
project

www.youngclergywomen.org